Home(is)lands

Home(is)lands

Home(is)lands: New Art & Writing
from Guåhan & Hawai'i

Edited by Brandy Nālani McDougall & Craig Santos Perez

an  press offering
Honolulu, Hawai'i

ala

means "basket" and "nest" in the Chamorro language and "path," "fragrance," and "to rise up" in the Hawaiian language. As such, we chose to honor our press with the name Ala because of our belief that literature has the power to carry, nurture, guide, beautify, and awaken. We publish a diverse range of styles in poetry, fiction, creative non-fiction, drama, graphic novels, and children's books by writers who trace their genealogies to the native peoples of "Polynesia," "Micronesia," and "Melanesia."

Brandy Nālani McDougall, founder
is Kanaka 'Ōiwi (Hawai'i, Maui, O'ahu and Kaua'i lineages) from Kula, Maui. She has over a decade of editing and publishing experience. She is the author of a poetry collection, *The Salt-Wind, Ka Makani Pa'akai* (Kuleana 'Ōiwi Press, 2008) and *Finding Meaning: Kaona and Contemporary Hawaiian Literature* (University of Arizona Press, 2016). She teaches Indigenous Studies in the American Studies department at the University of Hawai'i at Mānoa.

Craig Santos Perez, founder
is Chamoru from Guåhan (Guam). He has worked as Editor for the past ten years for various literary journals and publishers. Additionally, he is the author of three poetry books: *from unincorporated territory [hacha]* (2008), *from unincorporated territory [saina]* (2010), and *from unincorporated territory [guma]* (2014). He teaches Creative Writing in the English department at the University of Hawai'i at Mānoa.

Other ala press offerings

Nafanua, edited by Dan Taulapapa McMullin (2010)
Penny for Our Thoughts, by Kamehameha Students (2011)
Matamai2:Intersecting Knowledge across the Diaspora, by Pacific Islander Studies Students, edited by Kerri Ann Borja-Navarro, Richard Benigno Cantora and Andrew Fatilua Tunai Tuala (2012)
Afakasi Speaks, by Grace Teuila Evelyn Taylor (2013)
Squid Out of Water, by Daren Kamali (2014)
passages inbetween (is)lands, by Audrey Brown-Pereira (2014)
Sourcing Siapo, by Penina Ava Taesali (2016)

Introduction

Four thousand miles of ocean separate the Hawaiian archipelago in the Central Pacific from the Chamoru archipelago in the Western Pacific. The descendants of these islands have parallel, yet separate, genealogies: the Kānaka Maoli (Native Hawaiians) descend from Papahānaumoku and Wākea (Earth Mother and Sky Father), while the Chamoru people descend from Fu'una and Puntan (Ancestral Sister and Brother). Despite the distance between us, our histories and futures have become entangled as colonies of the United States.

European imperialism first invaded the shores of the Chamoru Islands in 1521 with the arrival of Ferdinand Magellan; three centuries of Spanish missionization, militarization, and colonization followed. Similarly, when imperialism invaded the shores of Hawai'i with the arrival of British explorer James Cook in 1778, British and American missionization, militarization and colonization followed. Despite efforts by Kānaka Maoli to maintain sovereignty, an oligarchy of transnational corporations colluded with the U.S. military to overthrow the Hawaiian Kingdom in 1893. The U.S. annexed Hawai'i during the Spanish-American War in 1898, despite the fact that the vast majority of Kānaka Maoli and other citizens of Hawai'i signed petitions against annexation. After the Spanish-American War ended and the Treaty of Paris was signed, Spain ceded the largest and southernmost island in the Chamoru archipelago, Guåhan (Guam), to the U.S., and sold the remaining northern Mariana Islands to Germany. After World War I, the northern Marianas became a Territory of Japan.

Our home-islands of Hawai'i and Guåhan were soon caught in the struggle for imperial control of the Pacific. On December 7, 1941, the Japanese military bombed Pu'uloa (Pearl Harbor); across the international dateline on December 8, 1941, the Japanese military also bombed and invaded Guåhan. While U.S. forces defended the larger military bases in Hawai'i, they abandoned and surrendered Guåhan. Japan's brutal occupation of Guåhan lasted for three years. In 1944, the U.S. reinvaded and successfully reoccupied Guåhan; in 1950, the Organic Act of Guam established the island as an organized, unincorporated territory of the U.S. and transformed Chamorus into U.S. citizens. In 1959, Hawai'i was incorporated as the 50th U.S. state, without any option given to its people for independence.

Under American colonialism, our peoples have suffered the ravages of disease, militarization, tourism, environmental destruction, and forced assimilation. Our languages, cultures, memories, lands, waters, and bodies have become endangered. The future seems bleak: the U.S. has declared the 21st century to be "America's Pacific Century"; at the same time, China has declared a coming "Asian Century" for the Pacific. Will Kānaka Maoli and Chamorus survive being caught in the crosshairs of such military, corporate, and imperial powers? As Kanaka Maoli poet, Wayne Kaumualii Westlake once wrote: "East / I'm afraid / Does not / Meet West— / they COLLIDE!"

Despite these legacies of violence and oppression, there is a rich and proud legacy of survival, resistance, political activism, decolonization, demilitarization, and cultural revitalization amongst Kānaka Maoli and Chamorus. From the Spanish Chamoru War (1671-1698) to the Kū'ē anti-annexation petitions, from Magalahi Hurao to Queen Lili'uokalani, from I Nasion Chamoru to the Hawaiian sovereignty movement, our peoples continue to fight for our sovereignty, at grassroots and international levels.

Literature, in its oral, written, and visual forms, has been central to Chamoru and Hawaiian social movements. In *Chamorro Self-determination/I Direchon I Taotao* (1987), editors Robert Underwood and Laura Souder write in the preface:

> [Chamorros] articulate, define and seek redress to issues not merely as participants in an American body politic, but

as members of an indigenous people whose cultural institutions predate any of the social, economic, and political institutions, which currently hold sway on [Guåhan]. This spirit has fueled the movement for Chamorro self-determination, inspired the artistry of the island's creative community, and motivated the quest for the return of stolen lands.

Similarly, one of the prominent leaders of the Hawaiian sovereignty movement, Haunani-Kay Trask, writes in her essay, "Writing in Captivity: Poetry in a Time of Decolonization" (1999) that contemporary Kanaka Maoli literature is "part of the resisting and reconstructing process" for the lāhui. She continues: "Whether we write *mele* (songs) or *oli* (chants) or essays or speeches or poetry or scholarship" there is "a continuing refusal to be silent ... Hawaiians are still here, we are still creating, we are still resisting."

Just as Chamoru and Kanaka Maoli social justice movements have inspired creative communities, so too have our writers and artists helped to inspire our social movements. Many of our writers have been actively involved in the sovereignty movement, using their literary and rhetorical skills to write and produce articles, letters to the editor, pamphlets, United Nations testimonies, interviews, speeches, documentaries, and protest signs. Of course, much like our ancestors who were resistant to the devastating processes of colonialism, much of Kanaka Maoli and Chamoru contemporary literatures is counterhegemonic, criticizing colonialism, militarism, and tourism; questioning colonial narratives and stereotypes; and articulating cultural identity, political independence, and visions of self-determination.

The literary and artistic works in this collection, written in 'ōlelo Hawai'i, fino' Chamoru, and English, examine the many historical and contemporary issues affecting our home-islands. The writers of Guam discuss the formation of social activism groups, testifying at the United Nations, language loss and revitalization, Indigenous Chamoru rights, the discourse of "Liberation Day," and the fight to save the sacred village of Pågat from being turned into a military firing range. The writers and artists of Hawaiʻi examine the desecration and repatriation of iwi kupuna (ancestral graves) amidst constant land development; voice resistance against the military and other forms of settler colonial occupation of sacred lands; honor the kūpuna for the knowledge given us in their stories; and celebrate the strength and innovation of our people to remain rooted in ancestral ways and yet adaptive and future-oriented. Woven together, this issue is a waʻa/sakman that gathers us together to emphasize our solidarity, mutually recognize our political and cultural sovereignty, and challenge American and Asian colonialism in all of its forms.

The importance of this work cannot be emphasized enough. As the prolific Samoan writer Albert Wendt writes in "Towards a New Oceania," "Self-expression is a prerequisite of self-respect." We deeply believe in this sentiment and would add, in the case of Guåhan and Hawaiʻi, that self-expression is a prerequisite of self-determination and that communal-expression is a prerequisite of sovereign communities. In speaking of the broader literary and political decolonization efforts throughout the Pacific, Wendt observes that our "artistic renaissance is enriching our cultures further, reinforcing our identities/self-respect/and pride, and taking us through a genuine decolonization; it is also acting as a unifying force in our region."

We are Hawaiʻi. We are Guåhan. Though Hawaiʻi is incorporated as a state, and Guahan remains unincorporated as a territory, we recognize these imposed titles to our lands and peoples as transient and momentary, especially when compared to the long and proud sovereign histories of our peoples. In the meantime, we will continue to support each other and fight for our sovereignty as long as we have breath.

Prutehi yan difendi.
Ua mau ke ea o ka ʻāina i ka pono.

Works Cited

Souder, Laura, and Robert A. Underwood, eds. *Chamorro Self-Determination: The Right of a People, I Derechon I Taotao.* Micronesian Area Research Center Educational Series no. 7. Mangilao, Guam: University of Guam Chamorro Studies Association, 1987.

Trask, Haunani-Kay. "Writing in Captivity: Poetry in a Time of Decolonization." *Inside Out: Literature, Cultural Politics, and Identity in the New Pacific.* Eds. Vilsoni Hereniko and Rob Wilson. New York: Bowman & Littlefield, 1999.

Wendt, Albert. "Towards a New Oceania" *Mana Review: A South Pacific Journal of Language and Literature* 1.1 (1976): 49-60.

Westlake, Wayne. *Westlake: Poems by Wayne Westlake.* Honolulu: University of Hawai'i Press, 2010.

Contents

...ʻāina Hānau... (detail)

April A.H. Drexel

...look what they've done...

April A.H. Drexel

in flagrante delicto (excerpts)

April A.H. Drexel

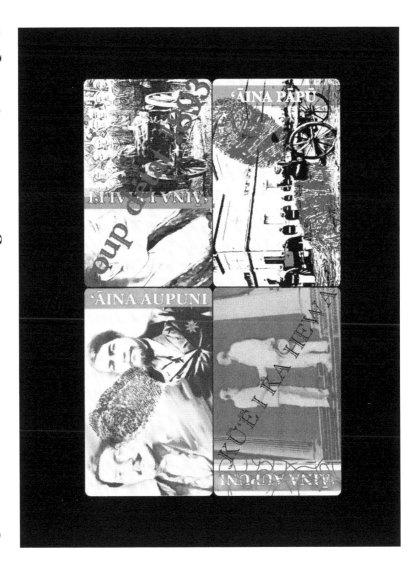

15

ancestral memory markers #2
April A.H. Drexel

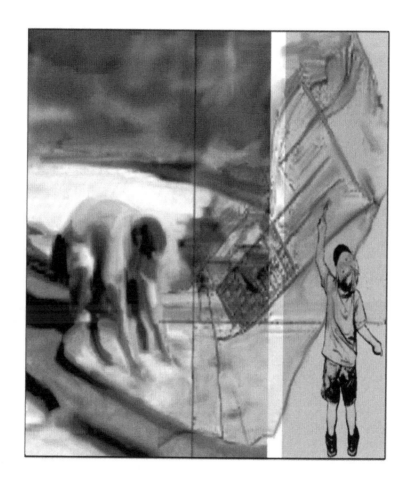

Selina Onedera-Salas

Gokña

Oh, Sainan-måmi as Fu'una
Un chule' i tataotao-ña as Puntan
Ya un fa'tinas i tano' gi pappa' i addeng-måmi
I lago'-ña fuma'tinas i tasi yan i hanom,
I lasås-ña fuma'tinas i inai yan i edda' ni' ayu muna'håhafye i te'lang i famagu'on-mu
guini gi iya Gokña

In hingok i katten-ñiha amnai ma yå'ho i anten-ñiha,
Ya manggaige ham guini på'go para in gagao dispensasion yan lokkue'
Para in na'fanangokko siha na hunggan,
Manggaige ham guini yan hunggan,
In hahasso siha.

Oh, Sainan-måmi as Fu'una
Pulan ham yan
Esgaihon ham mo'na gi i kareran-måmi…
I kareran i famagu'on-mu,
I famalao'ån-mu,
I hagå-mu siha guini.

17

Where are you from?
(Mānoa, New England, Ireland)
Because of Chantal Spitz

David Kealiʻi

And you bid us write

consider the language we use –

is this my mother tongue? Kēia koʻu ʻōlelo makauahine?

how my thoughts are shaped
by the language of a place I've
seen only as a tourist:
ʻo Pelekane.

"What is my nation?"
Said Heaney quoting MacMorris
with so many generations
and miles of sea between me
and the Ghaeltacht

so many layers
of
famine
salt water
iron crosses

this history I/we carry

and what can I do but learn?

And write back to wholeness.

Where Are You From?
(Son For the Return Home)
David Keali'i

Dwelling

Mine is a concrete kingdom
where steel and glass spire towards clouds
while below,
people lured by beach lines
and reinterpreted plantations
scatter their dreams through
grime and shine far and wide across the island.

Iwi

I know what lies beneath it all,
What is disturbed over and over.
I feel powerless
until others show me what it means
to stand up,
take responsibility for those who've passed on.
Their bones are our kuleana.

Community

The warmth,
the welcome home from other Hawaiians
knowing they mean:
"We will receive all who come back,
no matter how many generations may pass"

Name

"You're in the homeland now.
You can use your Hawaiian name."

'O Keali'i ko'u inoa."

Honi

This simple greeting and farewell
almost brings me to my knees.
Nose to nose
share: mana

Such simple beauty

This intimacy with other Hawaiian men
upon first meeting,
in a place constructed on
sterile masculinity,
tugs at my na'au.

I never knew
this was possible

Context

was always important
and now I understand
where I fit
where I make
the most sense.

Save Pågat

Jay "Sinangan" Baza Pascua

The jungle looms in the distance…a foreboding presence can be felt.

A haunting low and steady whistle drones as the wind whips through the leaves.

The sound almost rings in your ears…a kind of warning of things to come.

The crunch of dead leaves and tall grass beneath your feet add to the mix.

Your heart pounds faster and faster…and together it creates an eerie rhythm.

You look ahead and see the darkness of the wooded canopy approaches.

The gentle slope almost mocks your descent into an abyss of shadows.

Your parents, your uncles and aunties, all cautioned you about what's to come.

Your muscles tighten and strain to maintain its poise.

You descend further and are enveloped by the sense that someone is watching you.

The wind and the rustle cease…it is a deafening silence in the jungle.

Your heart beats louder now as you search your way through a maze of rock and trees.

The jagged limestone outcroppings of rock take the shape of ancient *togcha* or spears.

You are no longer in your domain…you have entered a world not yours.

You creep ever so slowly down the slope further into a chasm.

Just when you feel you can't take it any longer…the jungle opens up.

The sun's rays are a welcome feeling as it touches your face.

However, the calm is short lived as you feel more stares pierce the back of your neck.

You shake and shiver as though you were drenched in icy cold water.

You grab your bottled water from your bag and gulp as sweat beads down your brow.

The stories you heard as a child of the *taotaomo'na* weigh heavy on your mind.

The hair on the back of your neck stand on end and goose bumps appear on your arms.

Your body tells you to run but you are far down a cliffside ravine.

Your break is almost over but you are told there is a fresh water cave ahead.

The more you think about it the more you dread entering another recess.

Candles are lit inside the cave casting flickering strange figures all along the cave walls.

This is where your ancestors bathed, rested, drank and lived.

The water is cool and refreshing and your sweat now steams off your body.

You dread leaving this nature-made abode to enter the unknown.

You walk out of the cave, up an embankment and you are back under the jungle's wings.

Everywhere you walk you stumble across *lusong* or mortars …they are everywhere.

The thought of a *makåna* a Chamorro shaman mixing his medicine disturbs your psyche.

You again feel enclosed and walk towards what feels like a faint breeze.

You swath your way through thick brush and vines and finally break free.

The view is breathtakingly stunning…an archway and beneath is the ocean.

You are on the edge of a cliff smelling the salt air as waves crash against it.

You should never fear the jungle or your ancestors.

You should never fear this trek into Pågat.

You should never fear carrying on a legacy thousands of years old.

You should fear the loss of respect for the ancestors.

You should fear the loss of this sacred ground called Pågat.

You should fear the loss of a legacy thousands of years old.

Face fear in the face and protect this hallowed ground.

22

Nā Wiliwili o Pāʻula

Tammy Hailiʻōpua Baker

ʻŌlelo Hoʻākaka (Introduction)

Hana keaka, or Hawaiian medium theatre, marries the traditional practice of haʻi moʻolelo (storytelling) with the collaborative form of theatre. The theatrical performance of traditional stories in our native tongue perpetuates the values, beliefs and cultural practices of our ancestors while empowering a Hawaiian identity for this generation. For both performers and spectators hana keaka has been a means to reconnect to our language and our culture. These Hawaiian medium plays breathe new life into the past and provide a venue for the transference of cultural knowledge via the theatre. In my classroom at the University of Hawaiʻi at Mānoa I utilize drama to inspire language production and regularly script plays for curriculum to aid language study and enhance fluency in second language speakers of Hawaiian. "Nā Wiliwili o Pāʻula" is a short one-act play I wrote for the annual language celebration entitled Mūkīkī Wai nā Mamo o Mānoa held by Kawaihuelani Center for Hawaiian Language at UH Mānoa.

Traditional stories like "The Wiliwili Sisters of Pāʻula" were used by our ancestors to teach proper socialization to the youth. Although each story contains multiple lessons, a particular theme or value commonly transcends the story—aloha, or love, compassion, and empathy. This story instructs siblings to have aloha for one another in any circumstance lest they suffer punishment for their cruelty and hateful behavior. Each Wiliwili sister ultimately reaps the consequences of her deficit of aloha revealed in her merciless treatment of the elder sibling Moholani. This story also explains the origin of the ʻahi, or tuna, created when two female shape-shifters are chopped up after seducing Moholani's husband.

Nā Hāme‘e

(ma o ke kā‘ina o ka ‘ōlelo o nā hāme‘e)
WILIWILIPE‘APE‘A: pōki‘i o Moholani, he u‘i ‘ōpe‘ape‘a
WILIWILIKUAPU‘U: pōki‘i o Moholani, he u‘i kuapu‘u
WILIWILI‘OHE‘OHE: pōki‘i o Moholani, he u‘i ‘ōhule
MOHOLANI: ka hiapo, ka u‘i loa o nā kuāhine Wiliwili
KĀNE a MOHOLANI: makua kāne a Kauilamākēhāokalani
‘AHIKĀHULI: wahine kupua no ka moana kūlipolipo
‘AHIKAKANĀ: wahine kupua no ka moana kūlipolipo
KAMA: po‘e kama‘āina o Pā‘ula
‘ĀINA: po‘e kama‘āina o Pā‘ula
KUPA: po‘e kama‘āina o Pā‘ula
KAHU HĀNAI AKUA: akua ma Kūaihelani, ka ‘āina huna i ke ao
KAUILAMĀKĒHĀOKALANI: keiki a Moholani

Mokuna Mua

(Aia nā pōki‘i WILIWILI ma ke kahua e ho‘oma‘ema‘e ana
i ko lākou wahi noho. Kā‘alo maila ‘o MOHOLANI lāua
‘o kāna KĀNE i ke kahua me ka pūliki ‘ana kekahi i
kekahi.)

WILIWILIPE‘APE‘A
‘O Moholani ka wahine aloha nui ‘ia o kākou a pau.

WILIWILIKUAPU‘U
Ma muli paha o kona u‘i—

WILIWILI‘OHE‘OHE
Kā! Kona u‘i. He u‘i nō au!

WILIWILIPE‘PE‘A
(me ka henehene ‘ana o kona ‘aka) ‘O ia kā!

WILIWILI'OHE'OHE
'Ae, he wahine u'i nō au.

WILIWILIKUAPU'U
He u'i nō 'oe—

WILIWILIPE'APE'A
'O ka 'ōhule na'e!

WILIWILI'OHE'OHE
E Wiliwilipe'ape'a, mai hana 'ino mai ia'u! Kohu pūnana manu
mōkākī kēnā lauoho ou.

WILIWILIPE'APE'A
He lauoho nō na'e. 'A'ole like me kēnā pahu kani e kēnā 'ōhule.

(E ho'ā'o ana 'o WILIWILIKUAPU'U e ho'opio i ke ahi e
ulu nei ma waena o kona mau kaikua'ana. I kēlā me kēia
'ōlelo e puka ai, 'o ka ho'okokoke nō ia o lāua kekahi i
kekahi.)

WILIWILIKUAPU'U
E 'olu'olu—

WILIWILI'OHE'OHE
'O ia ho'i! A pehea lā kou 'ano o ka 'ōpe'ape'a?!

WILIWILIPE'APE'A
Pehea lā ho'i?

WILIWILI'OHE'OHE
Ke puhi mai ka makani, e kīlepalepa wale ana nō kou lauoho ma 'ō
a ma 'ane'i!

25

WILIWILIKUAPU'U

Ua lawa ka ho'opāpā 'ana e nā kaikua'ana. Mai hana 'ino kekahi i kekahi!

WILIWILI'OHE'OHE

'O ia ala nō ka mea i lele kāmoko ma luna o'u!

WILIWILIPE'APE'A

(iā WILIWILI'OHE'OHE) Nāu ka 'iniki mua!

WILIWILI'OHE'OHE

He aha kāu e kēnā ipu kai hinālea?

WILIWILIPE'APE'A

'Ele'elepī ka waha!

WILIWILIKUAPU'U

Kā! Ua 'oki! Ukiuki wale 'olua i nā mea a 'olua i 'ōlelo ai no ka u'i a u'i 'ole paha.

(Nānā lākou kekahi i kekahi.)

He u'i nō 'oe e Wiliwilipe'ape'a a he u'i nō ho'i 'oe e Wiliwili'ohe'ohe. He u'i kākou apau.

WILIWILIPE'APE'A

Pāwali mai ana kahi kaikaina kuapu'u o kāua.

(Pū'iwa 'o WILIWILIKUAPU'U i ia 'ōlelo a WILI-WILIPE'APE'A. 'O ka huli akula nō ia o WILIWILIKUA-PU'U me ka mākaukau e ha'alele.)

WILIWILI'OHE'OHE

E ke kaikaina.

26

(Kū ʻo WILIWILIKUAPUʻU. Hoʻohuli ʻo ia i kona kino holoʻokoʻa i mea e ʻike ai i kona kaikuaʻana ma muli o kona kuapuʻu.)

He ʻoiaʻiʻo kāu mea i ʻōlelo ai.

WILIWILIKUAPUʻU
Mahalo.

WILIWILIPEʻAPEʻA
ʻO ia nō! He uʻi kuapuʻu ko kāua muli a he uʻi—

WILIWILIʻOHEʻOHE
E hāmau e kēnā ʻōhumu kini!

(Hoʻi maila ʻo MOHOLANI.)

WILIWILIKUAPUʻU
(iā WILIWILIPEʻAPEʻA) He keu nō ʻoe o ke aloha ʻole!

WILIWILIPEʻAPEʻA
Auē, pinana kahi ihu.

MOHOLANI
He aha ka pilikia?

WILIWILIPEʻAPEʻA
ʻAʻohe mea e ka uʻi laʻahia!

WILIWILIʻOHEʻOHE
ʻAʻohe āu mea ma ʻaneʻi!

MOHOLANI
E Wiliwilikuapuʻu, he aha kai kupu ma waena o ʻoukou?

WILIWILIPE'APE'A

Holo peka.

WILIWILIKUAPU'U

'A'ole pēlā ko'u 'ano!

WILIWILIPE'APE'A

Pēlā nō—

WILIWILI'OHE'OHE

'A'ole pēlā!

WILIWILIKUAPU'U

Ho'opāonioni mau!

MOHOLANI

Ua 'oki! No ke aha 'oukou e hana 'ino mau ana kekahi i kekahi?

(Ho'i maila ke KĀNE a MOHOLANI.)

KĀNE a MOHOLANI

E ku'u hine, ku'u wahine u'i.

MOHOLANI

E ō e ku'u kāne.

KĀNE a MOHOLANI

I ka lae kahakai ana kēia.

MOHOLANI

'Ae. E kakali nō kēia i kou ho'i 'ana mai.

KĀNE a MOHOLANI

He ho'i mai koe. Ke aloha nui e ka ipo.

(Honi pū lāua.)

MOHOLANI
'Ae a hui hou nō kāua.

WILIWILI'OHE'OHE
(i nā pōki'i WILIWILI) E uhaele kākou.

MOHOLANI
E nā pōki'i, e alia iki mai.

(Huli lākou iā MOHOLANI a 'o ka pāweo akula nō ia.)

He aha kā 'oukou mea e pāweo nei?

(Hahai akula 'o MOHOLANI i nā WILIWILI.)

Mokuna 'Elua
(Aia nā wāhine kupua, 'o 'AHIKĀHULI lāua 'o 'AHIKA-
KANĀ, e 'ōlala ana i ko lāua mau kino i ka lā ma ka 'ao'ao
'ē a'e o ke kahua.)

'AHIKĀHULI
E 'Ahikananā.

'AHIKANANĀ
E ō e 'Ahikāhuli.

'AHIKĀHULI
He aha kēlā 'ala a'u e honi nei?

'AHIKANANĀ
He 'ala...he 'ala o ke kāne nō ia.

('Ike 'ia ke KĀNE **a** MOHOLANI e iho ana i ka lae kahakai.)

'AHIKĀHULI
'Ā'oia. Eia a'e ke kāne u'i i kipa pinepine mai i nei lae kahakai.

'AHIKANANĀ
'Oiai, 'a'ohe ona hoa hele—

'AHIKĀHULI
A he u'i maoli nō 'o ia—

'AHIKANANĀ
E lilo paha 'o ia i hoa no kāua.

'AHIKĀHULI
Hūi e ia nei!

'AHIKANANĀ
Hūi e kēnā kanaka nohea!

KĀNE a MOHOLANI
I 'ōlelo mai nei 'olua ia'u?

'AHIKĀHULI
'Ae. He mai e nanea pū me māua.

'AHIKANANĀ
E ho'omoe 'ia paha ka 'upena a nanea pū mai.

'AHIKĀHULI
E hō'olu'olu i kēnā kino luhi ou.

'AHIKANANĀ
(me ka ho'opā 'ana i ke KĀNE) Na'u paha e lomilomi iā 'oe.

KĀNE a MOHOLANI

'A'ole paha. I ka holoholo ana kēia—

(Ho'opili a puni 'o 'AHIKANANĀ lāua 'o 'AHIKĀHULI
i ke KĀNE a MOHOLANI.)

'AHIKĀHULI

E holoholo pū me māua-

'AHIKANANĀ

I ka moana kūlipolipo.

KĀNE a MOHOLANI

A- A- 'A'ole.

(Ma kahi 'ao'ao o ke kahua 'ike 'ia nā KAMA'ĀINA, 'o
KAMA, 'o 'ĀINA a 'o KUPA, e nānā ana i ka hana ma ka
lae kahakai.)

KAMA

'A'ole anei kēlā ke kāne a Moholani?

'ĀINA

'O ia nō. He aha kāna hana?

KUPA

He aha lā ho'i? Me he mea lā, e lilo ana nō 'o ia i kēlā mau wāhine
kupua.

KAMA

Ho'ohihi paha lāua i ka u'i o ia kāne?!

'ĀINA

'A'ole paha maopopo ke 'ano o ia mau wāhine i ke kāne.

KUPA

Oi hoʻowalewale mau nā wāhine kupua i kā haʻi kāne.

KAMA

A ʻo ka lilo akula nō ia o nā kāne iā lāua ala.

ʻĀINA

Pehea lā nā wāhine kupua o ka moana kūlipolipo?

KUPA

Pehea lā ke kāne a Moholani?

(Luliluli ko lākou poʻo me ka haʻalele ʻana aku. ʻIke ʻia ka hoʻowalewale ʻana o nā wāhine kupua i ke KĀNE a MOHOLANI ma kahi ʻaoʻao o ke kahua.)

ʻAHIKĀHULI

No laila, inā ʻoe e hoʻi pū me māua—

ʻAHIKANANĀ

E hoʻomau māua i kēia haʻi moʻolelo ʻana no nā kaʻao o ka moana

ʻAHIKĀHULI me ʻAHIKANANĀ

...kūlipolipo.

KĀNE a MOHOLANI

Malia paha—

ʻAHIKĀHULI

E luʻu nō ʻoe i loko o ke kai a—

ʻAHIKANANĀ

A hoʻi pū me māua i ko māua ana ma ka papakū o ka moana.

(ʻŌlelo hāwanawana nā wāhine ma kona pepeaio.)

KĀNE a MOHOLANI
'O ia paha.

'AHIKĀHULI
'O kō puni nō ia.

'AHIKANANĀ
I kāne 'oe na māua.

KĀNE a MOHOLANI
I kāne ho'i au na 'olua?

'AHIKĀHULI
'Ae, me he kāne 'oe na māua a me he mau wāhine māua nāu.

'AHIKANANĀ
He mele, he inoa no ka moana kūlipolipo,
Ka moana nui lipolipo ē,
Ka uliuli lipolipo o ke kai hohonu,
Hohonu ke kai o Kanaloa,
He loloa ke aloha ē.

(Mino'aka ke KĀNE a MOHOLANI a 'o ka lu'u nō ia
o lākou apau i loko o ke kai. Pio ke kukui.)

Mokuna 'Ekolu
('Ā maila ke kukui. Aia nō 'o MOHOLANI ke kakali aku
nei i kāna kāne ma ka 'ao'ao 'ē a'e o ke kahua. Ho'i aku
nei 'o ia nei i ka hiamoe a ala hou maila.)

MOHOLANI
Auē, ua wana'ao mai nei. Ma hea lā kahi kāne a'u?

(Kā'alo akula 'o MOHOLANI i ke kahua. 'Ike 'ia nā

KAMAʻĀINA e hoʻomākaukau ana i kā lākou mau pono lawaiʻa.)

KAMA

Aloha mai.

MOHOLANI

Aloha nō kākou.

KUPA

Aloha e Moholani. Pehea mai nei?

MOHOLANI

ʻO ia mau.

ʻĀINA

He aha kāu hana ma ʻaneʻi?

MOHOLANI

Kakali aku nei au i kuʻu wahi kāne ma ka hale a ʻo ka hoʻi ʻole mai-

(Nānā ʻo KAMA i kona mau hoa.)

No laila, ke ʻimi nei nō au iā ia ma nā wahi apau aʻu i ʻike ai.

KAMA

Ā...Iā mākou ma kahakai i nehinei, aia nō kāu kāne ma laila.

MOHOLANI

ʻO ia nō?!

KUPA

ʻAe. Luʻu aku nei ʻo ia ala i loko o ke kai.

MOHOLANI

A pehea?

'ĀINA

(kohu namu) A ua lilo paha kāu kāne i—

MOHOLANI

He aha kēnā āu i 'ōlelo mai nei?

'ĀINA

Aia nō paha 'o ia ma ke kai.

KAMA

Moholani, i ko mākou kuhi, ua lilo paha kāu kāne iā 'Ahikananā a
me 'Ahikāhuli.

MOHOLANI

Iā 'Ahikananā a me 'Ahikāhuli?

KAMA

(kimokimo ke po'o) 'Ae.

'ĀINA

'Ae.

KUPA

'Ae.

MOHOLANI

No ke aha? Pehea lā?

KUPA

Pehea lā ho'i, he mau wāhine kupa.

MOHOLANI

Mahalo.

KUPA

Aloha nō kahi kāne ʻauana wale aku!

Mokuna ʻEhā

MOHOLANI

Kā! Poʻe kupua, ʻino, ʻino wale! Hoʻowlaewale ʻia nō kuʻu kāne aloha!

(I ka puka ʻana o kēia mau ʻōlelo, huli akula ʻo MOHO LANI a hoʻokokoke aku ʻo ia i kahi o WILIWILIʻOHEʻOHE e noho ana.)

MOHOLANI

E Wiliwiliʻoheʻohe ē! Kū mai nei ē! E Wiliwiliʻoheʻohe ē! Kū mai nei ē! Ua ʻike paha ʻoe i kuʻu kāne i lawe ʻia e ʻAhikananā e ʻAhikāhuli? ʻIliʻili pekepeke, ʻiliʻili nehe.

WILIWILIʻOHEʻOHE

(me ke keu) ʻĒ! Kāne nui palaualelo! ʻAʻohe au i ʻike i kāu kāne!

(Haʻalele aku nei nō ʻo MOHOLANI me ka hāloʻiloʻi o kona waimaka i ka lua o ke kaikaina, ʻo WILIWILIPEʻA-PEʻA.)

MOHOLANI

E Wiliwilipeʻapeʻa ē! Kū mai nei ē! E Wiliwilipeʻapeʻa ē! Kū mai nei ē! Ua ʻike paha ʻoe i kuʻu kāne i lawe ʻia e ʻAhikananā e ʻAhikāhuli? ʻIliʻili pekepeke, ʻiliʻili nehe.

WILIWILIPEʻAPEʻA

ʻĒ! Kāne nui palaualelo! ʻO wai ka mea i ʻike i kāu kāne!

(Hoʻomau aku nei ʻo MOHOLANI i ka hale o ka muli loa
ʻo WILIWILIKUAPUʻU.)

MOHOLANI

E Wiliwilikuapuʻu ē! Kū mai nei ē! E Wiliwilikuapuʻu ē! Kū
mai nei ē! Ua ʻike paha ʻoe i kuʻu kāne i lawe ʻia e ʻAhikananā e
ʻAhikāhuli? ʻIliʻili pekepeke, ʻiliʻili nehe.

WILIWILIKUAPUʻU

ʻĒ! Kāne nui palaualelo! ʻAʻohe au i ʻike iā ia!

(Haʻalele akula ʻo Moholani me ka haʻuhaʻu ʻana. Hea
aku nei ʻo MOHOLANI i nā KAHU HĀNAI AKUA o kāna
keiki kāne.)

MOHOLANI

Auē, auē nō hoʻi ē. E nā kahu hānai akua o kaʻu keiki kāne, eia
nō au ke noi haʻahaʻa nei iā ʻoukou e hoʻokuʻu mai i kaʻu keiki, iā
Kauilamākēhāokalani i kōkua noʻu.

(ʻŌʻili maila ʻo KAUILAMĀKĒHĀOKALANI me kona
KAHU HĀNAI AKUA.)

KAHU HĀNAI AKUA

E Kauilamākēhāokalani, lohe mai nei ka leo kūmākena o kou
makuahine. E hoʻokuʻu nō mākou iā ʻoe e iho i kahi e noho ai
kānaka e kōkua aku i kou poʻe mākua.

KAUILAMĀKĒHĀOKALANI

Ua pilikia ʻia paha lāua?

KAHU HĀNAI AKUA

Lilo aku nei kou makua kāne iā ʻAhikananā lāua ʻo ʻAhikāhuli, he
mau wāhine kupua lāua o ka moana kūlipolipo. ʻImi aku nei kou

makuahine i kōkua nona mai kona mau pōki'i a 'o ke aloha 'ole mai...

KAUILAMĀKĒHĀOKALANI
Na'u e mālama.

KAHU HĀNAI AKUA
'Ā'oia. Ō hele 'oe.

(Iho akula 'o KAUILAMĀKĒHĀOKALANI i kahi o MOHOLANI e noho ana.)

KAUILAMĀKĒHĀOKALANI
E Māmā ē, lohe mai nei i kou leo uē!

MOHOLANI
E Kauila ē, ua lilo kou makua kāne iā 'Ahiknanā a me 'Ahikāhuli.

KAUILAMĀKĒHĀOKALANI
'Ae, ua lohe 'ia. Na'u nō e mālama. E iho au i kai e ki'i iā ia. Aia ā ho'i mai au, e ho'oponopono 'ia nā pōki'i kaikaina aloha 'ole ou!

(Kimokimo ke po'o o MOHOLANI me ka 'ae 'ana aku i kāna keiki kāne. 'O ka holo nō ia o KAUILA MĀKĒHĀOKALANI i kahakai.)

Mokuna 'Elima
(Ma kekahi 'ao'ao o ke kahua, e nanea pū ana nā wāhine kupua 'o 'AHIKANANĀ lāua 'o 'AHIKĀHULI me ke KĀNE a MOHOLANI. Ukiuki 'ino 'o KAUILA

MĀKĒHĀOKALANI i kona 'ike 'ana i kona makua kāne me ia mau wāhine.)

'AHIKĀHULI

Kīolaola kahi iʻa,
Liʻa mau i ka ʻono (o ka) līpuʻupuʻu,
ʻUʻu ē, ʻuwī ka nuku—

'AHIKANANĀ

He hoa kipa ko kākou.

'AHIKĀHULI

He aha ke kumu no ka huakaʻi ʻana mai e ke keiki uhelehe?

KAUILAMĀKĒHĀOKALANI

I hele mai nei au e kiʻi i koʻu makua kāne!

'AHIKANANĀ

Kou makua kāne?

'AHIKĀHULI

ʻO wai lā kou makua kāne?

KAUILAMĀKĒHĀOKALANI

ʻO ka mea a ʻolua e milimili nei!

'AHIKANANĀ

ʻAʻole kēia he makua kāne nou, ʻeā?

'AHIKĀHULI

He ipo aloha ʻo ia nei na māua.

KAUILAMĀKĒHĀOKALANI

ʻAʻole loa pēlā!

'AHIKANANĀ

ʻO ia nō kā hoʻi! E haʻalele ʻoe iā mākou!

39

'AHIKĀHULI
'A'ole loa māua e ho'oku'u ana i ka ipo laua'e a māua.

KAUILAMĀKĒHĀOKALANI
Mai 'au'a 'olua! E ho'oku'u mai nō i ko'u makua kāne.

'AHIKANANĀ
I ke aha ho'i? I ka 'ahakea!

'AHIKĀHULI
'Ā'oia! Ō hele 'oe e kēnā wahi ihupōhue!

(Kanalua ihola ke KĀNE a MOHOLANI. Pi'i a'ela ka huhū o KAUILAMĀKĒHĀOKALANI a loli a'e nei ke kino kanaka ona i kino uila.)

'AHIKĀHULI
Auē, pi'i ke kai.

'AHIKANANĀ
He kino uila!

'AHIKĀHULI
Ō ho'i kāua o papau pū auane'i i ka uila!

('Oaka ka uila ma ka lima o KAUILAMĀKĒHĀOKALANI i ka papakū o ka moana. I ia manawa nō i 'oki'oki 'ia ai ua maua wāhine kupua nei a paukūkū. Lilo a'e nei nā paukū i mau i'a. Mai laila mai i loa'a ai kēlā 'ano i'a, he 'ahi.)

KAUILAMĀKĒHĀOKALANI
No ko 'olua 'au'a loa, ua lilo 'olua i mau i'a. 'A'ole loa 'olua e ho'owalewale hou aku i kā ha'i kāne! (i kona makua kāne) E ho'i nō kāua i ka hale o kāu wahine e kaukau ana i ka minamina o kou lilo 'ana aku i kēlā mau 'ahi.

40

KĀNE a MOHOLANI
(me ka mihi) Auē, ua ʻuhene maila i ka mele a ʻo ka lilo akula nō ia i ua mau wāhine kupua ala.

KAUILAMĀKĒHĀOKALANI
Aloha nō.

(Hoʻi pū ʻo KAUILAMĀKĒHĀOKALANI me kona makua kāne i ka hale o MOHOLANI.)

Mokuna ʻEono
(I ka hiki ʻana aku o KAUILAMĀKĒHĀOKALANI me kona makua kāne i laila, puka maila ʻo MOHOLANI a me nā pōkiʻi WILIWILI ona.)

MOHOLANI
E kuʻu kāne, ua ola nō ʻoe!

(Pūliki ʻo MOHOLANI i kāna KĀNE a me kāne keiki kāne.)

KĀNE a MOHOLANI
(me ke kuhi ʻana i kāna keiki) Ola au iā ia nei. Nāna nō i hoʻopākele mai iaʻu.

MOHOLANI
Mahalo a nui iā ʻoe e kuʻu keiki, e Kauilamākēhāokalani.

WILIWILIPEʻAPEʻA
Kā! Ua hoʻi maila ke kāne nui palaualelo.

WILIWILIʻOHEʻOHE
ʻO ia nō, kāne nui palaualelo.

WILIWILIKUAPU‘U
‘Auhea lā kahi uhalena.

(Henehene ka ‘aka o nā pōki‘i WILIWILI.)

WILIWILIPE‘APE‘A
Auē, ua loa‘a paha i ka pīwa lena!

WILIWILI‘OHE‘OHE
Kahi ‘umeke pala ‘ole!

(E ho‘olohe mai ana ‘o KAUILAMĀKĒHĀOKALANI i ka ‘ōlelo a kona mau ‘anakē me ka haka pono ‘ana iā lākou.)

WILIWILIKUAPU‘U
(iā KAUILAMĀKĒHĀOKALANI) He aha kēnā āu e kauaheahe nei?

KAUILAMĀKĒHĀOKALANI
No ko ‘oukou aloha ‘ole i ke kaikua‘ana o ‘oukou, ko‘u makuahine, ‘o Moholani, he pa‘i mai koe.

(Henehene ka ‘aka o nā WILIWILI. Lapa ka uila mai ka lima o KAUILAMĀKĒHĀOKALANI a ho‘olilo ‘ia nā pōki‘i WILIWILI i mau kumu wiliwili.)

E Wiliwili‘ohe‘ohe ē.

(Lapa ka uila a pau ke kino wahine o WILIWILI-‘OHE‘OHE. Kū pa‘a nō ‘o ia me he kumu lā‘au lā.)

No ka ‘ōhule, lilo ‘oe i kumu lā‘au mā‘ohe‘ohe.
(Pū‘iwa a‘ela ka ‘ohana.)

E Wiliwilipe‘ape‘a ē.

(Iā WILIWILIPEʻAPEʻA i lohe ai kona inoa, hoʻomaka iho nei kona holo. A lapa ʻia ʻo ia e ka uila.)

E kīlepalepa mau ana kou mau lau i ke aheahe o ka makani.

(E huli ana ʻo WILIWILIKUAPUʻU me ka manaʻo o ka haʻalele ʻana aku.)

E Wiliwilikuapuʻu ē.

(Kūlou ihola ʻo WILIWILIKUAPUʻU a lapa ʻia e ka uila.)

E like nō me ke kuapuʻu, pēia nō ke kekeʻe o kou wahi kumu.

(Aloha aku nei ʻo KAUILAMĀKĒHĀOKALANI i kona mau mākua.)

KĀNE a MOHOLANI
E kuʻu hine aloha, ʻaʻole loa au e ʻauana hou. ʻOiai he keiki hoʻoponopono ʻole kā kāua, ke huhū iho.

KAUILAMĀKĒHĀOKALANI
E nā mākua, e noho nō ʻolua me ka maluhia aʻu i hoʻoponopono ai a mau loa aku.

MOHOLANI
Mahalo i kāu mau hana kupaianaha e kuʻu keiki.

KAUILAMĀKĒHĀOKALANI
(me ka honi ʻana) Aloha nui e ka makua.

MOHOLANI
Aloha nō.

(Pio ke kukui. Ua pau. Pipi Holo Kaʻao)

Inserting in History,
Alternative Process—Titas 1
Aata

Inserting in History,
Alternative Process—Titas 2
Aata

Inserting in History,
Alternative Process—Titas 3
Aata

Inserting in History,
Alternative Process—Titas 4
Aata

Inserting in History,
Alternative Process—Titas 5
Aata

Inserting in History,
Alternative Process—Titas 6
Aata

Returning to My Mother(is)land,
Returning Home
Kisha Borja-Kicho'cho'

I am a Chamoru woman in the 21st century
trying to find balance between change and continuity
attempting to stabilize what is left of my unstable

memories

memories which have triggered holes in my already traumatized soul
a soul suffocated by gated communities and hotels and "No Trespassing"
signs

all of which attempt to disconnect us from the one thing
we can still claim as ours.

But how can we call ourselves, i manaotao tåno'
the people of the land
if we have been misplaced and displaced
in our very own
home?

—Kisha Borja-Kicho'cho'
from "I am a Chamoru Woman in the 21st Century"

WHAT DOES IT MEAN TO BE CHAMORU?

*Cultural identities come from somewhere, have histories. But, like
everything which is historical, they undergo constant transformation.
Far from being eternally fixed in some essentialised past, they are subject
to the continuous 'play' of history, culture and power... [I]dentities
are the names we give to the different ways we are positioned by, and
position ourselves within, the narratives of the past.*
—Stuart Hall

Every Chamoru has different thoughts on this question,
and thus there are many definitions of what it means to be
Chamoru. Being Chamoru is to practice the Chamoru way of
life (inafa'maolek and Kostumbren Chamorro) and speak fino'
Chamoru (*Chamorro Heritage* 23; Souder 41-42). Being Chamoru
"is first and foremost being of Chamorro blood" (Souder 42).
"A Chamoru is a direct descendant of the original inhabitants of
[Guåhan...] not determined in degrees or fractions" (Santos, "I
Taotao Tåno`"). There are also the theories about the origin of
the word Chamoru itself. One common theory is that the name
is derived from the highest ranking Chamoru caste, the chamorri.
Another theory is that the name "Chamorro" was given by the
Spanish to mean shorn head because Chamoru men "did shave
their heads, leaving a small topknot on the crown" (Plaza 4).
Because of the debate surrounding the origin of the term, there are
Chamorus who have chosen to refer to themselves as Matao, which
was the highest class in pre-Spanish contact Chamoru society
(personal communication with Leonard Iriarte, July 2010; *The
Official Chamorro-English Dictionary*).
    Moreover, in the 1990s, there was much debate regarding
the spelling of the name of the Indigenous culture and people of
the Mariana Islands. Chamorus and non-Chamorus alike would
use one of the following spellings: Chamoru and Chamorro.
Proponents of each spelling had various reasons to justify which
was correct and should therefore have been made official.
Legislation was eventually passed which stated that "Chamorro"

would be the official spelling used in English documents, place names, buildings, and facilities (Taitano, "Kumision"), while "Chamoru" would be used in documents and items written in the Chamoru language (Today, however, many people use both of the spellings, regardless of the language being used in documents; I have chosen to use "Chamoru" throughout this essay). It is important to note that there is also a third spelling which Chamorus use: CHamoru.

I agree that "[t]he subject of Chamorro identity is rife with controversy" and that there is no one definition of what it means to be Chamoru (Souder 41). *Who* is considered Chamoru is also controversial, as the "Organic Act of Guam" (1950) granted US citizenship to "inhabitants" and their children (not just Chamorus) who resided on the island by April 11, 1899, or who were born after this date, thus implying that any ethnic group residing on the island after April 11, 1899 and before 1950 and their descendants could also claim the Chamoru identity and rights ("The Organic Act of Guam"). This has had negative implications on the Indigenous Chamoru community who traces their genealogy to before 1898 (in terms of Indigenous rights such as rights to lands and cultural practices).

I have asked myself what it means to be Chamoru many times since I arrived in Hawai'i in 2004. Before I left Guåhan, I never really thought about who I was as a Chamoru. I am both Chamoru and Filipino by ethnicity, but I grew up Chamoru, in a Chamoru household, learned Chamoru values, beliefs, and practices, went to a lot of Chamoru celebrations and events, and could recite the "Inifresi" and sing the "Fanohge Chamoru," a Chamoru pledge and the "Guam Hymn," respectively. Aside from the time when I attended a baptist school, I was surrounded by Chamoru people at parties, at the beach, at the stores, and most importantly, at home. While I grew up around fino' Chamoru, nengkanno' Chamoru, dandan Chamoru, taotao Chamoru, inafa'maolek, chenchule`, linamen (respetu), ginai mamahlao, oral traditions, my immediate and extended families, the tåno' and tåsi, and social and cultural events, which I strongly believe all helped to shape my Chamoru identity, they were never really articulated for or by me. What made me who I was as a Chamoru were never given names or definitions. I didn't think about being Chamoru; I just was Chamoru. My elders didn't define inafa'maolek for me; I was just taught to be a good person so that in turn, others would be good to me. My family gave chenchule' (mostly in the form of money or food) whenever we went to celebrations, rosaries, or funerals; and when people would come to our parties, they would reciprocate the gifts. Our Chamoru-ness was evident in our everyday actions. But just because my elders around me weren't sitting around a table with papers, pens, and computers, writing about and defining who we were, it doesn't mean that we didn't know who we were and that we weren't critical of who we had become. For example, I remember going to parties and having to manginge' my elders (even the ones I didn't know) because if I didn't, then I would embarrass myself and my family and would get spanked at home. There have also been several occasions where I would speak to elders in English, and they would ask, "Håfa? Ti siña hao fumino' Chamoru?" ("What? You can't speak Chamoru?"). I would look confused, and they could tell my answer was "no."

During that time, I wasn't too embarrassed because most Chamoru kids I knew couldn't speak fino` Chamoru. It wasn't "cool" then. We wanted to be good English speakers; we wanted to be like the kids on the American TV shows and movies. Chamoru kids who denied their Chamoru heritage and embraced the American culture and dream were commended by their peers. I even remember that when I was in elementary school, I used to tell my classmates that I was half Chamoru, half Filipino, and full English. Not knowing at the time that I was acknowledging a 200% identity, I wanted to somehow prove that even though I was one of the lone brown Pacific Islanders amongst the sea of haole and Asian kids at my baptist school, I was just as good as they were at English.

Those who spoke fino` Chamoru, or who spoke English but had a Chamoru accent, and didn't dress like the Americans, were regarded as "chaud." Chaud had a very negative connotation to it. To the Chamorus in the central part of Guåhan, chaud referred to those who were Chamoru and proudly showed that they were. It also referred to the non-American way some Chamorus dressed and sounded. From personal experience, while I was growing up, most Chamorus would say they were Chamoru, but they would never display their pride in the forms of physical objects such as stickers, t-shirts, and jewelry. This was mostly because if they did display their pride, they would be regarded as chaud, teased mostly by their own fellow Chamoru brothers and sisters for being proud of who they were culturally and for showing such pride. I didn't know it when I was a kid, but Chamorus' inability to proudly display their Chamoru-ness was a direct implication of their colonial conditioning. We could proudly hang and pledge to the American flag, post "We Support Our Troops" stickers and magnets on our cars and our refrigerators, and wear American clothes and jewelry, but we couldn't wear Chamoru jewelry and clothing, post up pro-Chamoru and pro-Guåhan stickers, or memorize and recite the "Inifresi" without being criticized and being called chaud.

Today, the term chaud still has a negative connotation. At least where I'm from on the island and the way that I continue to hear it being used, chaud has come to be used very loosely in everyday conversation, sometimes without justification. For example, if something is not visibly aesthetic (like clothes, a house, a car), Chamorus will dub the object as chaud. Chamorus also continue to call other Chamorus chaud for the way they sound (if they speak English with an accent or speak broken English) and the way they look (for example, if they wear yori and bahåki clothes in public). However, the difference between the time when I was a kid and now is that a Chamoru cultural renaissance seems to be occurring. Though I didn't live at home for six years, I did visit twice a year, and each time I came back, I saw more

Chamorus displaying their Chamoru pride. They would put "Chamoru," "671" (Guåhan's area code), and "Che'lu" stickers on their cars and trucks (even stickers with their last names and family names). They would wear Chamoru jewelry made of spondylus (spiny oyster shell which, when sanded down, turns into a bright orange color; worn mostly by Chamoru women) and clam shell (particularly the sinahi, the shape of the crescent moon, signifying the right time to fish and hunt; worn mostly by Chamoru men) which our ancestors carved and wore. They would design and wear t-shirts with Chamoru words (for example, "Fa'nu'i" and "Che'lu"). This movement is making its way to the Chamoru masses.

The display of Chamoru-ness hasn't come only in the form of objects, however. There are also more Chamorus participating in cultural events and hosting activities that focus on us, our culture (such as language revitalization), and our history. Though these same Chamorus who have been actively involved in this cultural revitalization might deny being considered chaud, many of us have indeed become what we were once ashamed to be. What we viewed as chaud were actually Chamorus who were just proud to be Chamoru and wanted to share their pride with others.

HU DIDINGU I TANO`-HU, HU DIDINGU I SAGÅ-HU (LEAVING MY ISLAND, LEAVING MY HOME)

Where speaks the knowledge of our ancestors? What of the ancient wisdom that has kept us alive for thousands of years? We must always remember that we are of an ancient people, and it is within ourselves that the spirit lives on. [...] We must not disregard our culture because once we lose insight into our past—once we allow ourselves to forget who we are—then we will forget where we are headed. And if we forget where we are headed, then we will no longer remember where we are from.
—Fanai Castro

It was during my first semester of college in Hawai'i that I started to question and reflect on who I was as a Chamoru. I was only "half" Chamoru. I couldn't speak Chamoru fluently. I didn't farm, fish, or hunt. I didn't eat red meat or pork (and have been teased by family and friends alike that I wasn't Chamoru because I didn't eat steak, ribs, Spam, and pig). I didn't have long hair. I started to think that people who were Chamoru had to look and act a certain way. I felt I wasn't Chamoru enough. I remember feeling so upset and lost because I didn't feel grounded; I wasn't secure with my Chamoru identity. I was beginning to reject and rid of my imposed Guamanian and American identities. *Who was I?*

Much of my uncertainty and insecurity had a lot to do with the fact that I was young, had just moved from everyone and everything I knew and the place I called home, and came to attend college on an island that seemed so much larger than Guåhan, with about nine times the amount of people. I lived on Kūhio Avenue, in the heart of Waikīkī, which was far away from Mangilao, the village where I grew up. To add to my culture shock, people would always ask me where I was from, who Chamorus were, what our culture was like, what the language sounded like. Many people would ask if Chamorus even had a language and culture because from what they had heard, our language and culture were practically dead. Though I did have a good grasp of my history and culture, I still felt I didn't know enough. I felt as if I always had to justify and defend my culture and my island. According to Chamoru scholar Dr. Robert Underwood, "Identity was not a problem for the Chamorros on Guam [...] until they were told it should be" (qtd. in Lowenthal 318). Below is a scenario of my experience of meeting people in Hawai'i for the first time and who knew nothing about Guåhan and Chamorus.

"Where are you from?"
Guåhan. [They give me a questionable look.] Guam.
"Where's that at?"
It's a really small island in the Pacific Ocean. It's about a

7-hour flight west from here; 3 hours from Japan.

[Some would even ask, "Is that part of the Philippines?"]

"So what do you call people from there...Guamese, Guamish?"

Well, the Indigenous people are called Chamorus. And people who aren't Chamoru but who were born and raised there call themselves Guamanian.

"What language do you speak there?"

Chamoru.

"How do you say 'hello' in Chamoru?"

Håfa Adai.

[laughs hysterically] "Haha, half a day, as in not a full day, but half a day!"

[This happens every time I tell people. I do feel offended, and I always think in my head, *No, you idiot! Actually, the first "a" in Håfa makes an "aw" sound.*

"How do you say 'goodbye?'"

Adios.

"That's like Spanish...'A-dee-os.'"

It's spelled the same as in Spanish but pronounced differently.

"So you all are Spanish?"

Well...there are a lot of Spanish influences in the Chamoru culture, such as Catholicism, our last names, and in our language. Spain ruled Guåhan for almost 400 years.

"So are you part of the Philippines?"

I HAGÅ´-HU, I MANGGAFÅ-KU, I HALE`-HU, I TANO`-HU (MY BLOOD, MY FAMILY, MY ROOTS, MY ISLAND)

To remove a people from their ancestral, natural surroundings or vice versa, or to destroy their lands with mining, deforestation, bombing, large-scale industrial and urban developments, and the like, is to sever them not only from their traditional sources of livelihood, but also and much more importantly, from their ancestry, their history, their identity, and from their ultimate claim for the legitimacy of their existence (Hauʻofa 468-469).

By 2007, I had the desire to be reunited with my mother tongue, to be reconnected with finoʼ Chamoru. After studying English all my life (and becoming really good at it—I was an English major, English tutor, and an editor) and Japanese for seven years, and after living away from home, a big part of me felt I needed to re-learn the language I once knew while in my mother's womb.

It is said that language is the carrier of culture. I had used Chamoru words and phrases in my poetry and everyday conversations, but I had yet to fully speak and understand the language. Since that time I realized how important it is for me to know the language of my people, I have been on a journey of rediscovery. This journey, this yearning for discovering who I am as a descendant and inheritor of an over 4,000-year old nation, led me to absorb as much finoʼ Chamoru as I could. While on Guåhan during breaks from school, I would go to Chamoru chant practice (I Fanlalaiʼan, led by Leonard Iriarte), read the "Juan Malimanga" comic strips and the "Finoʼ Chamoru" lessons in the *Pacific Daily News* (Guåhan's local newspaper), listen to KISH 102.9 (the Chamoru music radio station), and beg my dad to speak to me in only Chamoru (which was his first language). In Hawaiʻi, I would try to use Chamoru in my poetry and read copies of Chamoru stories from home.

When I started attending UH-Mānoa in 2008, I felt even more of an urge to speak and understand Chamoru, as I had gone to the 10th Festival of the Pacific Arts in American Sāmoa and was inspired by all of the Islanders who could speak in and understand their respective languages. So while in graduate school, I audited the Chamoru language class every semester and forced myself to use it in my writing, in emails, on facebook, in text messages, and in daily conversations.

Like many other Indigenous peoples, it took for me to leave home in order to appreciate my culture more and to appreciate who I was as a Chamoru. Today, I am not fluent in speaking Chamoru, but I can understand and speak it enough to get by in a conversation. And though I strongly agree that my knowledge and fluency of fino' Chamoru can contribute to the perpetuation of Chamoru culture and the continuity of our people, I do not believe that our language is the sole definer of who we are as a people. But Chamorus often judge one's Chamoru-ness based on language fluency alone. In addition to language fluency, many Chamorus judge the Chamoru-ness of others based on whether or not they fish, farm, or hunt, whether or not they carve and wear "traditional" Chamoru jewelry, whether or not they're Catholic (because majority of the Chamorus are), where they're from in the Mariana Islands (Chamorus themselves often say that those from the Northern Marianas are not as Americanized as those from Guåhan and are thus more Chamoru), if they've been born and raised elsewhere, and the grand separator of our people, who has more blood than whom.

While raised on Guåhan, I didn't have the opportunity to live off of the land or the sea. My family and I didn't have land to farm on nor did we live by the ocean. My tåta (my dad's father) did raise chickens and pigs at his house and cows at a nearby ranch (which he didn't own). And my parents did grow tumates, green onions, donne', lemon, mangga, and pugua' behind our house. But I myself did not cultivate or harvest anything. And as much as it disappoints me that I wasn't raised to live off of the land and the ocean, I am motivated to start doing so.

I am continuing to discover who I am as a Chamoru, who Chamorus are in general. Many of us share similar nostalgic stories of getting flicked in the ear, pinched in the chachaga`, or spanked in the dågan when we were naughty; going to all the gupot—gupot umasagua (fandånggo), fiestas, lisåyu, and interu—and praying and eating Chamoru food (red rice, barbeque chicken and ribs, chicken kelaguen, potato salad, roasted pig, and latiya);

playing endless card games and eating canned food (especially Spam, corned beef, and vienna sausage) after a typhoon, when there's no power or water for weeks; going to mom and pop stores to buy pickled papaya and mangga, pickles, rokill, and bottles of King Car; and strolling around the island. These were some of my experiences growing up as a Chamoru on Guåhan.

I might not speak the language fluently (I will get there). I might not farm or fish (I will get there). I might not ever know all things Chamoru (I hope to get close). But this does not mean that I am not Chamoru or that I am less Chamoru than those who can do these things.

In Hawai'i, I helped to start the Håfa Adai Club while attending Hawai'i Pacific University, hoping to meet other Chamorus from the Marianas and to share our culture and history. While at UH-Mānoa, I helped to reinstate the Marianas Club, inspired by my Chamoru language class and the club's predecessor, the Chamoru Club (which was defunct in 2004) (personal communication with Brant Songsong, August 2009). A few friends and I also started Fight for Guåhan to address issues related to Chamoru culture and politics on Guåhan. This is how I displayed my pride for my culture while away from home and how I dealt with not living at home.

Today, I wear my spondylus and ifit jewelry. I am committed to becoming fluent in fino' Chamoru. I continue to work on projects that promote the Chamoru language and culture (such as through the children's television show "Nihi!"). I have a daughter named Lina'la' (means life) who is my daily reminder that, for her, I must remain strong in my Chamoru identity.

I know now that Chamoru isn't just who I am ethnically and culturally; Chamoru is the way I live out my everyday actions. I will continue to remember my past, take care of my island and my people—even when things get difficult—and practice my culture.

As a Chamoru of the 21st century, my identity crisis (also known as my journey of rediscovery) has been quite the experience. I have finally come to embrace my Chamoru-ness. At the same time, I still wonder where my journey of rediscovery will continue to take me. I will always love pickled mango and papaya, fiesta food, and dandan Chamoru. I will practice inafa'maolek and chenchule' and will show respect for my elders. Yet this doesn't mean that I will reject all things non-Chamoru. I still love hip hop, baked ziti, and editing papers. But I will always be Chamoru, no matter what anyone says, and I can define who I am as a Chamoru in my own way. In the words of Black feminist, activist, and writer Audre Lorde:

> [I]t won't matter particularly whether you are or I am a Black poet lesbian mother lover feeler doer woman, it will only matter that we shared in the rise of that most real and threatening human environment, the right to love, to work, and to define each of us, ourselves. (157)

I am from Guåhan. My blood is from this land. My family is from this land. My roots are in this land.

I moved back to Guåhan in 2010. After six years of being away, I had to reacquaint myself with my island and my people, rediscovering, relearning, and reclaiming my Chamoru-ness. I know that they remembered me. They knew that I was of them. They knew that I was home.

Works Cited

Castro, Fanai. "Coming into Consciousness." *GU-Guam's Life in Print*. Jan./Feb. 2006. Issue No. 3. 16-18. *Chamorro Heritage— A Sense of Place*. Hagatna, GU: Department of Chamorro Affairs, 2003. 23-44.

Hall, Stuart. "Cultural Identity and Diaspora." *Colonial Discourse and Post-Colonial Theory*. Eds. Patrick Williams and Laura Chrisman. New York: Columbia UP, 1994. 392-403.

Hau`ofa, Epeli. "Pasts to Remember." *Remembrance of Pacific Pasts—An Invitation to Remake History*. Ed. Robert Borofsky. Honolulu: UH Press, 2000. 453-471.

Lorde, Audre. "Self-Definition and My Poetry." *I am Your Sister—Collected and Unpublished Writings of Audre Lorde*. Eds. Rudolph P. Byrd, Johnnetta Betsch Cole, and Beverly Guy-Sheftall. New York: Oxford UP, 2009. 186-187.

Lowenthal, David. "Mobility and Identity in the Island Pacific: A Critique." *Mobility and Identity in the Island Pacific*. Eds. Murray Chapman and Philip S. Morrison. Wellington: Victoria UP, 1985. 316-326.

The Official Chamorro-English Dictionary—Ufisiåt na Diksionårion Chamorro-Engles. Hagåtña, Guam: Department of Chamorro Affairs, 2009.

"The Organic Act of Guam." Hinasso': Tinige' *Put Chamorro—Insights: The Chamorro Identity*. Agana, Guam: Political Status Education Coordinating Commission, 1993. 52-65.

Plaza, Felicia. "Origin of the Word Chamorro." *Guam Recorder*. 1.1 (1971): 4-5.

Santos, Anghet Leon Guerrero. "I Taotao Tano'." *The Tribune*. 2 Nov. 1991.

Souder, Laura Marie Torres. *Daughters of the Island—Contemporary Chamorro Women Organizers on Guam*. 2nd ed. Maryland: UP of America, 1992. 40-42.

Taitano, Gina E. "Kumision I Fino' Chamorro/Chamorro Language Commission." 2009. 3 July 2010. <http://guampedia.com/kumis ion-i-fino'-chamorrochamorro-language-commission/>.

Glossary

bahåki: house/work clothes; non-dressy clothes
chachaga': inner thigh
che'lu: sibling; could also refer to a close friend ; not gender specific
chenchule': reciprocal gift-giving, mostly in the form of money or food
dågan: buttock
dandan Chamoru: Chamoru music
donne': hot pepper
fa'nu'i: to show, present, demonstrate
fino' Chamoru: Chamoru language
gai mamahlao: to have shame; this is a very important practice because if one were to be tai mamahlao (without shame), then s/he could embarrass her/his family
inafa'maolek: loosely translated as interdependence, reciprocity
Kostumbren Chamorro: the blending of pre-contact Chamoru practices and customs with introduced Spanish and other influences and practices
linamen: respect
mangga: mango
manginginge': kissing the right hand of an elder as a sign of showing respect; this is done when greeting an elder and again when leaving (an event, mass, a party); it is also done after the recitation of the rosary
nengkanno' Chamoru: Chamoru food
pugua': beetlenut
tåno': land
taotao: person
tåsi: ocean
tumates: tomatoes
yori: slippers

New Contact

The following [static] based on actual events or people.

TAKE PHOTO

of her
sparkle in her
face two holes her
first is black, deep like her
grandmother swimming with eels her
second is black, wide, and shallow like her
uncle's pond he built when she was still a mermaid her
small breasts were mistaken for jewels she was attacked for her
sparkle in her.

SHARE PHOTO

Itchy. To show her off. Tap-tap-tap. New album. "Wet," he told them. "Check it out." Spreading his photo around. But. "What the hell is that, bro?" Someone pointing. Others started pointing. Too. Zoom. His thumb and pointer finger. Spreading, spreading. "Is that her skin?" "Rash?" "Looks like a fuckin' fish." Spreading. They've heard your pointer can fall off. Itchy, itchy, itchy.

COMMENT

First skipped message
"It's me. Uh. I gotta talk to you. Something…I found something. Call me back."

Next message
"Where are you? I've been calling [static] touch with you. I know [static] something to do with this – [static] come from me. Now you fuckin' call me back!"

Next message
[static] A heavy object dragging. [sobbing] "I'm sorry [sobbing] I'm so sorry. I'd take it back, I'd take it back if I could [sobbing] I was a little boy – it was a mistake. [static][an inaccurate list of names] and you were [sobbing] sparkling."

SEARCH HISTORY

alpha	self-lubricating	pattern of attack	pointer
spreading	faint discoloration	small breasts	forgotten
susceptible	tongue for mosquitoes	bad romance	said brochure
when wet	when well-fertilized	privacy settings	kingdom come
I told you	let cry for three days	instead of jewels	egg-laying

An Interview with Cara Flores-Mays

Tell us about yourself. Who are you? Where are you from? What is your educational and/or vocational background?

My mother is a native of Guam. She met my father while attending college in the states. They had two chamaolie babies (my older sister and I) and moved us back to Guam before I turned 2. I spent my childhood years in Guam and moved to Michigan when I was 12 so that my mom could obtain her doctorate. Still, I always considered Guam "home". I moved back with my daughter (now 6) almost 6 years ago so that I could care for and spend time with my grandmother before she passed. I hail from the south-central part of Guam (Talofofo).

I went to school at a small college in Michigan called Andrews University. I graduated with a degree in digital media in communications (BT). After graduation, most of my work revolved around media/marketing/strategy for smaller companies and specifically for non-profit work. I do other stuff in my spare time, too. Like hike, write, play my piano, zumba...

How did you get involved with We Are Guahan and what is your/ the group's goals/dreams?

We Are Guåhan came together after the DEIS was released in November 2009. Initially, it was a group of folks who came together to read the DEIS. I thought that I was just going to help with some of the resource/marketing (flyers, graphics, etc) stuff. But after reading some of the DEIS, I was so disgusted that I kind of threw myself into organizing and educating. Back then, it seemed that We Are Guåhan was the only group putting out accurate information about what the DEIS really said. And it was important stuff: life-altering, irreversible, destructive.

On a very practical level, We Are Guåhan just wants our community to have enough information to make an informed decision. We are also completely committed to protecting the things that are important to our community.

For a long time, the question posed by people in support of the buildup was: Do you want Guam to prosper?

And, of course, people said yes. And so, the question "Do you want the military buildup?" and "Do you want Guam to prosper?" became one in the same.

The EIS made folks realize that there was more than just one question to answer. Do you want over-crowded schools? Do you want environmental destruction? Do you want the cost of homes and rent to go up? Do you want homelessness to increase? Do you want to further stress the public health system? And that's all that we really wanted... was for people to have the full story and not just part of it.

On a more idealistic level, We Are Guåhan wants three things:

1. a sustainable Guam;
2. an informed community; and
3. that our community determines our future, that it's not something that just happens to us, that we have to cope with.

What do you feel has been the relationship between literature and the decolonization movement in Guahan? Has literature been an important part of We are Guahan's work?

Our literature is our voice and our story which is important because our story has been told by others with their preconceived ideas or for their own personal gain and sometimes we believe their version of our story because we've heard it for so long. But more often, we don't hear our story at all. Our story is important. Literature is one way to communicate that.

We Are Guåhan is only a small part of the movement and there are a bunch of other folks who are paying attention to the literature of our movement and doing really well at it. We actively support all efforts to tell the people's story. Unfortunately, WAG has spent a lot of time reading some very poor literature like the EIS, other official reports and studies (and some editorials in the PDN). This type of literature benefits the movement because it isn't ours. When we quote the EIS and other official studies and reports, we aren't making a biased statement; we're quoting facts and figures that have been released by folks who are often biased *towards* the buildup. Folks demand that we show studies and figures to support our claims (that the buildup as currently proposed costs more than it will bring in, will hurt our environment and stress our schools and public health system, will further damage our language and our culture) but when folks make claims about the buildup being good for Guam they don't have to support their claims. And they can't. We've read all of the un-biased reports and studies and it doesn't say that anywhere.

What are the major barriers to Guahan's social movements? What future projects does We are Guahan have in mind to create a sustainable Guam and an informed and empowered community?

I think that most major barriers to anything in life are self-imposed. I mean, we'll always be up against corruption, greed, limited resources, and 24-hour days. Our movements must be broad and diverse. There are so many possibilities in that. I'm more overwhelmed by the possibilities than by any of the barriers. I'm really excited about We Are Guåhan's next few months. We're soon releasing the first in a series of educational videos, we're polling candidates on community issues before the upcoming elections, and we have a few projects in the works that promote sustainability -- keep an eye out! I think one of the most important projects that we're working on right now is the GAPSS (Guam Alumni of the Public School System) Program which is a college prep program for Guam's public high schools. Last year we awarded 29 SAT scholarships. This year we're expanding the program to help high school students with the college application process. We'll also be bringing college prep and financial aid workshops into the high schools. Our primary goal is to empower students and remove the obstacles to higher education by filling in the gaps.

MCBH
Ashlee Lena Affonso

Fourteen years old and I am afraid to walk to the store.
Whistled at like a delectable piece of meat.
Military men always looking to score.
The same faces,
the same attitude.
Everything about these soldiers
is the same.
My sister, twelve years old,
the same hungry eyes follow her path.
These men are serving who?
A country, or a need?
Staring at the back gate of the
Marine base.
Private access.
The same men going
In and out.
In and out.
In and out.
Protection for who?
From who?
They've never made me feel safe.
They have made me into the enemy.
Driving up and down my road.
Like they own it.
They own nothing.
Nothing.

Hawaiian Tourism Authority

Ashlee Lena Affonso

The Hawaiian Tourism Authority
Is leading the people of Hawai'i
Into a quicksand pit.
We keep slipping into this notion
That we will be financially okay,
Indefinitely.
In this movement to save
a drowning economy
Our mentality of life
Has been so ill-construed.
Buried deep in the realm of capitalism,
We willingly suffocate ourselves and
Lose grasp of our culture
In the pursuit of the American dream.
We have lost sight of our self worth.
Experience the beauty of these islands
Through a website that unlocks the
Secrets of the past.
Play in legendary Waikīkī,
View the wrath of Pele
On the Island of Moku o Keawe.
It is our pleasure to serve you.
E Komo Mai.

Gå'pang's Quest

Michael Luján Bevacqua

Up the grey peak, where the earth belches fire and coughs smoke
Beneath his feet, the grass is withering as the earth breathes through the dirt
Browning and blackening, slowly being choked of green as he rises higher along the path
Before him is the maw, the mouth of the earth, cracked rocks, frozen fangs
Within, coiled within the grasp of a shriek-bringing beast
Is the skull of his great father, the finest spear and strongest shield of his line
The pride of his faraway village
Even in death, his skull was a cup of bone, filled with power and fortune
The warriors who drank his dreams were never crushed in battle

Two moons ago it was stolen from his house
The roof aflame and the smoke skyward the mocking trail of the honor thief
Gå'pang had taken his canoe with the first wink of the sun and following north
Moons passed but the smoke always stayed ahead, whispering away
But always shouting again in boldness as the thief struck again
For all these moons the creature remained smoke and ash
Only known through the crushed remains of its violated victims
Toasted corpses and roasted villages connecting like stars in the sky
Even now as he stands before the lair of the enemy

The lurking stealer of others' glory
He can only guess as to the form his foe will take
Fire will be his blood, a scaly scalded skin beast that spits human torment
He will have no words, his voice will be in flame
He will have no tongue, but a spear made from the earth's blood

As he sank his canoe into the black sands of this land
And prepared his weapons for what waited above
He was blessed to find a great elder turtle
Beached with its ancient soul, breached only its shell remaining
Hardened by several lifetimes worth of waves
And smoothed to a surface that no man could scratch
The shell shield was a heavy haul
But it would defend him in ways nothing else could
Reaching almost his height, he could crouch cower behind it
Safe from fire fangs and crushing claws

Before he enters the thief's maw
He looks to the sky, fingerlengths of skylight, dancing through
Thick grey clouds full of doubt and doom
He calls upon those who came before
Those who fought before and died before

And became the bones that filled the homes of their families
Those whose arms and legs became the stabbing blades
That he bears lashed to him in battle
Oh Great Fathers who stared into the fearsome sun and did not blink
Oh Great Fathers who fought in silence in nothing but moonlight
Oh Great Fathers who fought to keep alive the line that pumps my blood
Give me the soaring strength that sent your rivals fleeing
And the demons of the day and night flailing in cringing fear

I am Gǎ'pang! He screams into the deepening blackness of the cave
I have stalked thee Honor Thief across islands and mountains
To see that the miracle of my father's father's father be returned
Give it to me or feel the bone blades of all my great fathers
Drink glory from your gutting
I am blessed by all the strung together signs that have led me to your lair
The stars of my ancestors have linked together to weave waves to bring me here
I will not leave without the honor of my village in hand
And what bag of scales you call a head tied to the mast of my ship

The blackness breathes
And the walls glow red with each breath
The mountainside rips, cracking pieces, shaking loose

As gasping laughs escape from the earth's maw

You are Gǎ'pang, and your quest is far from complete
I am the gasher, I am the stomach slitting slasher
I am the teaser of flesh, the teacher of pain
I am the claws that are sharpened by the boasting words of weak legged mortal morsels
With the vanity of you and your long chewed to carnage father hanging fat in the air
My claws glow and shine now, skin slicing moons in my night-like cavern
Come too close and you will witness them slice the stars of your ancestors from the sky and crush you
with their falling
Your bone blades will drink me
In the same in which your foolish fathers would dare to quaff the ocean
Dare to drink me and I will rip the jaw from your mouth and flush eyes from your skull
I will burst you with my wrath

For many breaths there is no noise from the two
The earth shakes, the grey clouds move
The bravery of his bones weakened, Gǎ'pang pauses
What grand monster waits within this earth door
He cannot win if he enters the dark, where this beast finds its own comfort
He knows he must lure it out

He calls out to the blackness,
I and the host of my fathers laugh at this nonsense
That a worm like you, caressed in your cave
Can slice anything, or gash anything
A worm like you waits for a foot to complete it
A worm like you waits for a thumb to measure it
You are a stain in the dirt full of shit, choking on wishes of glory
I have spat upon you and given all your dreams the flavor of my morning meal

The black mouth within a mouth yawns wide
The dark mixing with fire
Stretching things terrible and soon to be seen
And the great beast escapes
Shooting forth from the earth
As flame froths from his lips
Gǎ'pang holds aloft his blessed shield
Watching fire fingers edge themselves around his defense
The air screaming heat and burning his eyes
The shield holds, the spirits are with him
His body bleeds fearful sweat, their cooling touch he hopes is more than death-water,
But instead the stone and bone of his fathers surrounding him

A voice, booming as if hollowed out and flowing from a channel into the womb of the earth.
Charcoal for the fire
An eye to the sun
Bones that I will crunch and become stuck between my happy teeth
As I lick your sacred parts loose moons from now
And I will always remember the taste of your pride

The fire fades, fireflies of ashes fluttering about
The quiet is anything but a cure for the madness of the moment
The shield protects but also restricts his view
He looks to the earth, ears straining to hear what his eyes cannot see
The dark sands before him, churn and groan
Claws kicking up a war song
The warning is lost as the wall before him begins to burst
The deep brown of his shield,
Laced with all the lost colors of the sea
Seems to panic as a horde of scratching can be heard on the other side
The shield that would not flinch as the bowels of the earth were poured upon it
Starts to shiver as claws sharper than killing stones begin their work
Feeling his shield begin to bend, Gǎ'pang retreats
He steps back, drawing forth two blades, gifts from his father

The shield tumbles and is crushed beneath a fearsome weight
The elder turtle's shell snapped and splintered to create a seat
For the terror-stenched honor thief
A towering lizard, whose scales are painted in slashes
Stained with a coat of earth-womb
Armor linked with darkened tones, no doubt from former failures of foes
Mountain blood pumped through it
Filling patches of darkened death drunk skin with hidden fire
Its head blooms the brightest, and the earth blood from its limbs
Flows forward to the point from which
Between curving menacing lips it could spill out
Like an army of heated death that would rain melting sling stones upon all

His defense gone Gä'pang surges forward
Only an audacious attack could bring town a foe of such height
Smoke escaping from every hole in that evil grinning head
With his mouth opening
An ocean of screaming boiling blood appears within
Straining, bubbling preparing to spray forth
His hand gripping around the once leg of his father
Whose tip had been sharped and blessed to never fail when sunken into flesh
He buried it in the gleaming neck of the beast

The shriek that slithered from that wound
Made the clouds, readying and rumbling swollen with the sky's tears pause
It filled the air, with the sound of a thousand murdered souls
Cheering on the quivering, squirming end of their murderer
The beast's blood, flowed out from the wound, taking the great blade of his father with it
Heating it to a bright glorious white, before swallowing it in melting gurgling death
The creature's own pride gushed out in a glorious river
Gashing like heated stones across Gǎ'pang's arms
The warrior jumped back, watching the neck and the will within
Struggle to keep aloft the great raving skull
In rage, Gǎ'pang could see the enemy's last eyes shimmering
The coming end pooling the hottest fire inside
Turning his evil skull into a cauldron, cooking whatever slimy, scaly soul it possessed
When the hovering head finally fell and struck the dirt
The earth sighed, a sign of relief
The bone thief's molten fire leaked out, sinking into the ground around it
Returning the blood of the earth to its eager mother

Into the black he went
Stumbling through piles of fallen warriors
Those who fought well, filled with the courage of their ancestors
And those who cowered and begged

All became human sticks and clubs scratched and scrubbed white in defeat
The bones clicked and clanked their thanks, fallen into praying mounds near his feet
Spirits filled the black so densely, the lines normally naked to the living
Hummed and shone, swirling with thousands of waving lights
All leading him to a skull, peering down half buried in dirt
And there, Gä'pang found his honor and the honor of his village

Note

This is a work of fiction: although it contains many factual elements of Chamorro history and culture, it is not meant to provide a solely historical view of our past. This is a creative work meant to use historical knowledge along with artistic imagination to give energy and vibrancy to our Chamorro pasts.

In 2009, I wrote a post on my blog *No Rest for the Awake,* titled "The Five Ayuyu Generals of Southern Guam." I described my enjoyment of the KOEI video game series *Dynasty Warriors,* whereby players get to control historical characters from China's Three Kingdoms Period and vanquish their foes on the battlefield. Although the game is filled with warriors blessed with supernatural skill and mythical might, the action is all rooted in historical personas and events. The title of my post came from the "Five Tiger Generals of Shu," which were considered to be some of the greatest warriors of the time and are still re-imagined in art today close to two millennia later.

When I look at Chamorro culture today and our collective memory, the way we organize our ancestral pasts, I want us to give similar life to our pasts. Recollections of our ancient pasts are dominated by only a few limited forms of representation: chanting and dancing. Part of the problem with these

81

representations is that they remind us of the past, which is valuable and important, but they also keep the past chained in particular forms. I want the past to live and breathe and join us today as something that is far more than just faded photos or uncertain stones in the jungle.

In addition, I dream of a day when Chamorros will organize their identity around heroic figures from their own culture and people and pasts. Chamorros today seem to identify with heroic figures from the White imaginary: presidents, "frontier" icons, movie stars, and fictional characters. Why don't we do more to rebuild our own heroic pasts, our own larger-than-life figures who will continually be reimagined and have their stories told in different ways? Why don't we do more to carve our own space in this world instead of continually cramming ourselves into someone else's imagination and dreams?

One could argue that Chamorro history was not written down until recently, whereas China has had an extensively archived history. This is of course nothing but *tåke' karabao*. Chamorros in fact have a very rich oral tradition that captured everything in the same way, in lengthy epic poems, songs and stories that captured their long histories and the exploits of their ancestors. Current lack of knowledge regarding our rich history is a result of Chamorros making choices, colonial choices, of giving up that history, replacing it with other things, and leaving their past faded, *sin kulot, taila'la'*, and thus *taisetbe*. There is no government agency which dictates that which we remember or that which we value. We make choices, and usually we make the easiest choices, and so people tend to follow whatever is on TV, or whatever is taught in school, or whatever most people around them seem to think. So of course we'd all act as if America is our past, present and future, because that's what everything around us seems to tell us.

We do not give our history the place, the life in our own lives, that it deserves. We know that ancient Chamorros lived a certain way, or that Chamorros under the Spanish lived a certain way, but where are our stories of them? Where is our famed storytelling ability when it comes to breathing life into these eras?

We act as if we are a people belonging to anthropologists and historians, when in reality what we need is simply to live, breathe, and remember our history as if we are believers, as if we are artists, as if we are Chamorro. Our history is not an abstract passage from a book to be memorized and then forgotten. Our Chamorro pasts are stories, paintings, poems, that are constantly being written, by us, and then forgotten, also by us. Whether our history gets longer and more textured, more nuanced and more full of life, or becomes stale, *måfñas*, empty, and meaningless, depends upon what we do ourselves.

It is up to us, all of us, as "everyday artists" together with a history that needs to be revitalized to name these ghosts of our past that we find haunting our closets, our car bumpers, tables at the Chamorro Village market, or refrigerator doors during Chamorro month. And we must give them monuments, spaces, memories, and stories as well.

Håfa i lini'e'-ta anggen ta atan mo'na pat tåtte para i estorian i mañainå-ta? Malefiåyon na acho' yan ti mahungok na estoria? Kao gaila'la' pat taila'la' i hale'-ta siha? Anggen taila'la', taimanu na siña ta na'gaila'la' siha? I na'manman yan ti hongge'on na estoria put i fuetsan i taotao-ta? Este diposti unu na estoria taiguihi.

Michael Lujan Bevacqua
Mongmong, Guam
May 2015

When Ilocos Norte became Luzon became Philippines (an Aegean string) became ink drained from skin . . .

Lyz Soto

— They have creams
for that you know —

The darkening spot:
a convection inhabiting the face
the window face
the side of my face always graced
by the sun.

— But I always wished
I was browner —

Racially spotted:
where I live as a darkening limb
no one can see my curdled hide
separate.

— And I always worried
about someone's feelings
getting hurt —

Across the sea hugging a coastal rim they forced islands into a nameable
chain . . .

named their colors garish
called their table a humble platter
bleached their garments
sold uniforms to all our kind
grind new words on the mill of their tongue

84

— Those feelings were never
my own —

Last night I dreamed in genetic string
these islands were not buried so deep
in this heap of absent flesh
so even strangers recognized an Ilocano hand
scrawled across my face
and knew I
did not imagine her.

The Power of Literature and My Experiences at the United Nations

Alfred Peredo Flores

Colonialism and globalization in Oceania have forced Chamorus, Hawaiians, and other native Pacific Islanders to leave their ancestral homelands in search of economic stability, expanded educational opportunities, and satisfactory health care (deGuzman, Flores, et al 149). These and other factors have created diasporic native populations throughout the world. As a diasporic Chamoru who has lived the majority of his life in California, literature has been one of the ways in which I have connected with the history and culture of my ancestral homeland of Guahan. For the majority of diasporic Chamorus, the economic recession that began in 2007 and the high cost of airfare have made it difficult to visit family and friends back home (the average round trip ticket from Los Angeles, CA to Guahan costs $2,000). However, literature is a powerful cultural medium that transcends geographic and constructed borders. It also has the power to influence the way a person understands the world and can help shape their identity. As a historian, I have utilized literature to connect with Chamorus in Guahan and throughout the diaspora.

As an early graduate student, literature provided me an opportunity to learn more about the historical and contemporary impact colonialism has had upon Guahan and its people. Literature was also an important part of my early intellectual development since my first trip to Guahan was not until 2007, when I was 27 years old. However, the work of Pacific Islander scholars such as Julian Aguon, Epeli Hau'ofa, Chris Perez Howard, Peter R. Onedera, Laura Marie Torres Souder, and Robert A. Underwood helped inform my foundational understanding of the United States militarization. Their work was informative and helped motivate me to become an advocate for the decolonization of Guahan. This essay discusses how my experience as a petitioner at the United Nations is connected to Chamoru and Pacific Islander advocacy and literature.

My Time at the United Nations

In October 2010, I traveled to New York City to testify before
the United Nations Special Political and Decolonization Committee.
Also known as the fourth committee, this branch of the United Nations
was created in 1961. Its main goal is to make recommendations to
the U.N. general committee regarding the decolonization of non-self
governing territories (United Nations 1). The purpose of my testimony
was to bring attention to how the U.S. military's proposal to relocate
U.S. Marines from Okinawa to Guahan was rooted in the historical
militarization of the island. Before my official testimony took place, I
decided to experience the sightseeing opportunity that New York City
offered. As a first time visitor of New York, my curiosity led me to visit
Ellis Island, the Empire State Building, the Statue of Liberty, and Wall
Street. While it was interesting to visit all of these places I had only
seen in movies or on television, the Statue of Liberty left the deepest
impression on me as I thought about my upcoming testimony. The irony
behind Lady Liberty is that it was given to the United States as a symbol
of America's commitment to the principles of democracy and freedom.
In reality, the U.S. government's evolution into a modern nation-state
has only resulted in the reproduction of colonialism at home and abroad.
As a historian, I have studied how certain principles of freedom do not
apply to indigenous people living within the borders and territories of the
United States. Thus, my experience at the United Nations reinforced my
understanding of U.S. colonialism.

For many years, Chamorus have traveled to New York City to
testify at the United Nations. Since the 1960s, the Special Committee
on Decolonization's responsibility has been to review the "political,
economic and social situation in each of the remaining non-self-
governing territories on the United Nations list" (United Nations 6). Part
of this process includes having annual hearings that allow petitioners to
voice their concerns over various issues impacting the non-self governing
territories. The Special Committee then submits its recommendations to
the General Assembly, who is supposed to implement those suggestions.
In 2010, I partnered with a delegation of researchers, teachers, and
community organizers to represent Guahan.

This group was formed through a network of Chamoru advocates
and activists who had worked together on other projects that supported

decolonization. Among the group were Chamoru graduate students Josette Quinata from the University of Southern California and Michael Tuncap from the University of California, Berkeley. Allies MyLinh Nguyen, Dave Roberts, and Maria Roberts also joined our delegation. I knew being a petitioner was important because I was following the legacy of Chamoru elders such as former Guahan Senator Hope Cristobal, Maga haga of the *I Nasion CHamoru* Debbie Quinata, and others who began this fight for decolonization in the 1960s and 1970s. As Chamoru scholar Laura Marie Torres Souder has discussed, Chamoru women have played a prominent role in the preservation of culture and in the advocacy for political self-determination (Torres-Souder 1-4). Unfortunately, my experience at the United Nations paralleled the social and political marginalization that other Chamorus experienced as petitioners at the committee hearings.

  The day of the testimony was chaotic and unorganized for unknown reasons. It could have been due to the challenges in organizing several dozen petitioners or it could have been due to the fourth committee's ambivalence in preparing all of the delegates. As a first time petitioner, I was overwhelmed with the lack of direction in the process of testifying. Tuncap, who had petitioned on several other occasions, told me he believed "the process was rooted in a complex form of colonialism that tokenizes indigenous petitioners" (Tuncap). In many ways, his belief underscored how I felt as a speaker. Luckily, I was able to rely on my fellow delegates who helped prepare me. When the hearings began, I quickly noticed that some of the U.N. representatives from various countries seemed uninterested in the testimonies and were also unwilling to engage with petitioners before and after their statements. After each petitioner presented their testimony, the committee chair allowed representatives to ask questions. Unfortunately, none of the representatives asked questions or made comments based on the testimonies that were given. This silence has led me to believe that the hearings are simply a ceremonial act of decolonization. Furthermore, I found their ambivalence to be frustrating because I thought it was a wasted opportunity for representatives and audience members to learn more about the colonial situation in Guahan and in other territories. Instead of using this opportunity as a learning moment, some of the U.N representatives were more concerned with checking their Facebook profiles or playing on their cell phones as in the case with the representative from the United States. While some representatives demonstrated their disinterest through social media, other committee members demonstrated much more obvious acts of disrespect.

Some members from the fourth committee conducted themselves in a manner that was more egregious than using their cell phones. During Josette Quinata's testimony, the committee secretary constantly whispered and smiled to the committee chair. This happened two or three times over the course of Quinata's four-minute testimony. It is unknown what the committee secretary was whispering about but I interpreted their actions as insulting, especially since the majority of the petitioners travel hundreds or thousands of miles on their own financial accord to express their concerns. Thus, my experience at the United Nations only reinforced an unequal colonial relationship that exists among the petitioners and the U.N. officials.

During my testimony, I also experienced the same unprofessional treatment that Quinata endured. After seeing their offensive behavior, I became angry. My discontent resulted in an aggressive reading of my testimony, as I wanted to the committee to feel my anger through the sound of my voice and my words. Similar to other petitioners, my statement concluded without any questions being asked of me. Afterwards an unknown woman told me, "I enjoyed your testimony. Your delegation always gives passionate testimonies." Her words made me think about how my testimony was part of a larger legacy of Chamoru advocacy at the United Nations. For example, in October 2009, the Guahan delegation was abruptly informed that petitioners would have to shorten their testimonies from seven to four minutes (Tuncap). During Hope Cristobal's testimony, U.N. officials attempted to stop her on several occasions after she had elapsed her four minutes. She vehemently refused and completed the reading of her entire testimony. All of the following Guahan petitioners followed her lead and also read their full testimonies. It was listening to these stories that made me realize that all of our testimonies are connected in an effort to achieve decolonization. After my delegation completed their testimonies, another significant moment occurred during the testimony of a single petitioner from the U.S. Virgin Islands.

Edward Browne's statement on the U.S. Virgin Islands was important because it linked the colonial situation in the Caribbean to the Pacific. In addition to discussing how Denmark and the United

States were responsible for the colonization of the U.S. Virgin Islands, he also referenced how Japan and the United States needed to resolve their colonial governance with the people of Guahan. What is most significant about Browne's testimony is that his reference to Guahan proves that colonized people throughout the world are cognizant of each other's colonial experience. His testimony was poignant because it reminded me of Julian Aguon's essay in his book, *The Fire This Time: Essays on Life under U.S. Occupation*. Specifically, Aguon argues that Chamoru survival is based on coalition building. He states, "Solidarity is not our best bet. It is our only one. As an international gathering of peace and justice activists, we are building momentum for the global demilitarization movement" (28). Browne's testimony and Aguon's essay reminds us of the importance in creating and maintaining a global network of advocacy among all people who live in colonized places. The solidarity among all people is greatly needed once we realize how the governance of these areas is inextricably connected. As Pacific Islander scholar Epeli Hau'ofa states, "acting together as a region, for the interests of the region as a whole, and above those of our individual countries, we would enhance our chances for a reasonable survival in the century that is already dawning upon us" (42). Hau'ofa's claim also supports that the political fates of colonized places remain deeply connected and that our survival is predicated on coalition building with other people and places.

Conclusion

My experience at the United Nations has been instrumental in my intellectual development and has fostered my commitment to the decolonization of Guahan. Even though my participation did not result in any tangible policy change, I encourage all people from non-self governing territories to serve as a petitioner at the United Nations. Testimonies given at the United Nations are documented evidence that prove Chamorus and other people have and continue to advocate for the decolonization of non-self governing territories. It is possible that if people stop serving as petitioners, U.N. officials will believe that decolonization is no longer needed. Furthermore, I believe it is instrumental for people to engage in various forms of advocacy. I argue that a multifaceted approach that includes creative writing, grassroots organizing, public education, research, and teaching will help promote and bring visibility to the experiences of colonized people. Moreover, these forms of agency will also encourage people to join the cause, as in the case of how literature has helped cultivate my political consciousness.

Even though Chamorus have endured a legacy of colonialism, they also have a legacy of survival. This spirit resonates in Chris Perez Howard's *Mariquita* and Peter R. Onedera's *CHeffla gi I Manglo'* (Whistle in the Wind). *Mariquita* is a biographic story that discusses Mariquita's life as a young woman living in Guahan during the 1940s. Like other Chamorus, the Japanese military forced Mariquita to live in a labor camp and subsequently killed her. In *CHeffla gi I Manglo'*, the main character named Nono' and his family utilize whistling as a warning system to avoid Japanese soldiers who are ransacking the homes in their village. In the end, Japanese soldiers capture Nono' and his family, who are then killed for their resistance. Even though both of these stories have tragic endings, they are a testament to the strength of the Chamoru people. As Chamorus continue to oppose American colonialism, their rights for self determination may one day become a reality.

UNITED NATIONS SPECIAL POLITICAL AND DECOLONIZATION COMMITTEE (FOURTH COMMITTEE)
October 5 & 6, 2010
Where the Past Meets the Present: The Historical and Contemporary U.S. Militarization of Guahan

Introduction
New York City, NY

Hafa Adai distinguished members of the United Nations Special Political and Decolonization Committee (Fourth Committee) and Chairman, H.E. Mr. Chitsaka Chipaziwa. I thank you for the opportunity today to discuss some of the issues affecting Guahan. I would especially like to recognize the committee members who have demonstrated their commitment to democracy by their attentiveness to the testimonies given today. I urge the committee members who have not been as attentive to these testimonies to follow the lead of your dedicated colleagues.

My name is Alfred Peredo Flores. I am a doctoral student in the Department of History at the University of CA, Los Angeles and a native Chamoru. I represent UCLA's Graduate Coalition of the Native Pacific, a campus organization committed to the advocacy for Pacific Islander issues at UCLA and its surrounding communities. As an historian, my research specifically examines the issues of land, labor, and immigration.

History's Utility to Contemporary Issues

Many people believe history is only important in understanding the past. Others believe the function of history is to provide an interpretation of historical events, people, and processes. In actuality, history is much more dynamic then simply studying the past. It provides an opportunity to understand how and why a nation or group of people has developed into its contemporary form. Thus, the history of a society and its people is not divorced from its contemporary manifestations.

As some of you may know, Guahan is being prepared for one the largest military expansion projects in U.S. history. It is estimated that 10,000 marines, their 8,000 dependents, and 10,000 temporary workers will all be brought to Guahan as a result of American military expansion. As an historian, I can tell you that this build up will have significant consequences that will permanently affect the island and its people.

Historical Context

Before I discuss the contemporary issues, I must remind the committee that this is not the first time Guahan and its people have experienced a military expansion of this magnitude. During and after World War II, the United States invested millions of dollars into transforming Guahan into an island of war (*Life* 63). This included the construction of Andersen Air Force Base and several military installations throughout the entire island. By 1948, the U.S. government owned 42% of the land on Guahan (Carano and Sanchez 336). In an attempt to expedite land acquisition, the U.S. government "cut corners in appraisals and in legal technicalities" (Rogers 216). In some instances, Chamorus were forced to relinquish ownership of their land with little or no compensation. In addition, the United States recruited thousands of people from Asia, the United States, and the Pacific Islands to work as civilian laborers for the military. The result was a multi-tiered wage scale that placed migrant workers and native Chamorus at the lowest end of the scale, while American workers received the highest wages, regardless of their duties (Carano and Sanchez 327-330). Finally, the environmental impact of U.S. militarization during the Cold War era has resulted in the permanent transformation of Guahan's environment. The construction of buildings, runways, and training areas has transformed rich farmland into permanent military structures. Even if the U.S. military returned these areas, they would be useless for self-subsistence activities since the land has been altered with concrete and steel.

Contemporary Issues

The next question is: How is the Cold War militarization of Guahan, related to the proposed militarization project facing the island and its people? The similarities are uncanny. You can replace the Cold War hysteria with the War on Terror. Instead of containing communism, the U.S. government is waging a war on terror. Furthermore, the U.S. military has discussed the possibility of needing more land for the creation of training sites, storage facilities, military family housing, and military installations (Limtiaco). The source for this land would most likely come from the Government of Guahan or from local landowners (just like the Cold War era). Moreover, the United States has already begun recruiting private companies and taking bids for military construction contracts. In turn, these companies will justify paying migrant workers lower wages due to their non-American status, making them susceptible to exploitive labor conditions (Jimenez). Since these companies will be subcontracted by the U.S. military, the Guahan Department of Labor will most likely not have the jurisdiction to oversee that proper working conditions, adequate lodging, and fair wages are provided to these laborers (similar to the Cold War era). It is most likely that these workers will be subjected to a hierarchical wage scale similar to that of the Cold War period. Finally, the construction of new military installations and buildings will permanently alter Guahan's physical environment. For example, the U.S. military is currently proposing to use the ancient village and burial site of Pagat to build a live-fire ammunition complex, consisting of multiple firing ranges. If this proposal comes to fruition, machine gun fire and grenade explosions will decimate Pagat. Thus, historical burial sites, artifacts, and the indigenous flora/ fauna will be permanently lost. Pagat is just one example of the possible consequences U.S. military expansion will have on the environment.

Ultimately, the continued militarization of Guahan will only perpetuate the United States' colonization of the island and its people. This will be due to the fact that the United States will not invest millions of dollars into developing it for warfare, only to return sovereign power to the Chamorus. If anything, it will only perpetuate the U.S. government's control over the island. This is evident by the military buildup that occurred during the Cold War era, which has resulted in the U.S. government's tightening control over the island and its people today.

Recommendations to the United Nations

My final recommendations for correcting these issues are the same suggestions made by the entire Guahan delegation today. I would like to emphasize to the Fourth Committee to thoroughly investigate the administering power's noncompliance with its treaty obligations under the Charter of the United Nations to promote economic, social, and cultural wellbeing on the island. Since treaties are suppose to be the highest law of the land, agreements a nation or people make, should be treated judiciously. Thank you for your time and consideration.

Works Cited

Aguon, Julian. *The Fire This Time: Essays on Life Under U.S. Occupa tion.* Tokyo: Blue Ocean Press, 2006. Print.

deGuzman, Jean-Paul, Alfred P. Flores, Kristopher Kaupalolo, Christen Sasaki, Kehaulani Vaughn, and Joyce Pualani Warren. "The Possibili ties for Pacific Islander Studies in the Continental United States." *Amerasia Journal* 37:3 (2011): 149-161. Print.

Carano, Paul and Pedro C. Sanchez. *A Complete History of Guam*. Rutland: Charles Tuttle, 1964. Print.

Hau'ofa, Epeli. "The Ocean in Us." *We Are the Ocean: Selected Works*. Honolulu: University of Hawai'i Press, 2008. Print.

Howard, Chris Perez. *Mariquita: A Tragedy of Guam*. Hagåtña: Cyfred, Ltd., 2000. Print.

Jimenez, Cher S. "Into the Breah Again: U.S. Looks to Filipinos." At times.com. *Asia Times*, 17 Nov. 2006. Web.

Life. "Guam: U.S. Makes Little island into Mighty Base." 2 July 1945: 63-75. Print.

Limtiaco, Steve. "Military May Retake Land." *Pacific Daily News*. 28 Sept. 2006. Print.

Onedera, Peter R. *CHeffla Gi I Manglo'* (Whistle in the Wind). Guam: U.S. Library of Congress, 2006. Print.

Rogers, Robert F. *Destiny's Landfall: A History of Guam*. Honolulu: University of Hawai'i Press, 1995. Print.

Torres Souder, Laura Marie. *Daughters of the Island: Contemporary Chamorro Women Organizers on Guam*. Lanham: University Press of America, 1992. Print.

Tuncap, Michael. Personal Communication. 5 Oct. 2010.

United Nations. *United Nations and Decolonization*. New York: United Nations Department of Public Information, 2001. Print.

The Lay Netters
Michael Puleloa

Jason Murayama says the Miloli'i fisherman stood alone behind a podium in the Grand Pīkake Ballroom of the 'Ilikai Hotel. The fisherman wore a dark t-shirt, jeans, and rubber slippers, and because of that, he didn't look like any of the other attendees at the conference, not even the other Hawaiians.

Jason wore a Reyn's aloha shirt and a pressed pair of fitted slacks—the clothes had been graduation gifts from his Moloka'i uncles. He felt impeccably dressed. He says when the Miloli'i fisherman took to the podium, he was sitting in the ballroom and looking down at new wingtip shoes—the incandescent light from a giant chandelier hanging in the center ballroom reflected off the polished black leather of his shoes like the rays of a sun, he thought.

He sat in a row of fifteen chairs that ended at an isle in the center of the room and then began again so there were fifteen more beyond that. He was in the forty-fifth row of fifty, nearly eighty yards away from the fisherman. There were men and women in all but a few of the seats in the ballroom. All in aloha attire. Some wearing lei.

The fisherman was going to be the last speaker before lunch, Jason says. He hadn't learned much while sitting there that morning. He was bored. And that made him anxious. There was really nothing he had learned about fishing. Only that speakers at fisheries conferences can sometimes drone on about hypothetical situations that have nothing to do with the lives of people like him. By this time, Jason says, he was waiting it out. He'd heard there was going to be an elaborate lunch buffet after the last speaker.

When the Miloli'i fisherman finally began to speak, Jason says he immediately looked up from his shoes. He hadn't expected anything would bring him back to the podium, but now he was intrigued. The fisherman was a thin man, in good shape, and from what Jason could see, there was nothing about him that might make him think he wouldn't see the man fishing somewhere off the Moloka'i coastline.

Most of the other attendees, Jason says, were older than him. The people around him looked thirty and forty, so he must've connected with the fisherman in part because the fisherman looked pretty young, too.

Jason was a fisherman. Or he had been. Now he was living on Oʻahu, attending a university. Living without a boat.

When we were younger, Jason was groomed by his uncles, so he knew plenty about the ocean. Whenever families on Molokaʻi had big parties, they always sent someone to see him. The families had known Jason's uncles, and over time, they had come to know Jason, too. His mother had been a Luʻuhine before she married Murayama, and on Molokaʻi, the name Luʻuhine was synonymous with fishing. All the Luʻuhine were fishermen, and the brothers, Jason's uncles, they knew their stuff, especially when it came to laying net. There were times, in fact, when the uncles had been visited by university researchers who spent days or weeks and sometimes a summer to learn about Molokaʻi fisheries.

Jason was young, still in grade school, when his parents took him to his uncles, Paul and Brian. They asked the uncles to teach Jason. The brothers were the best, the parents said, and Jason was a smart boy, ʻeleu, and naturally inclined when it came to the ocean. But the brothers told the parents, no, it wasn't a good idea, that they'd be too rough on the boy. It was just their way.

The Miloliʻi fisherman began to tell a story, Jason says: When the fish arrive, he said, he wakes his five-year old son at four and gets him dressed before breakfast. He hands his son lunch in a bag. It's just him and his son. His wife, she watches the daughters. She wakes up later and takes them to school. His son is young, but he doesn't complain. In fact, the fisherman thinks it was the son's idea the first time the son went fishing with him.

For the most part, the crowd at the conference listened intently, Jason says. But some attendees stood up to leave. They cradled binders and notepads and other conference handouts as they filed out of the aisles.

His son, said the fisherman. The boy reminds him about gas and ice because he knows before he came, the father used a canoe. They walk to the shoreline before any sign of the sun. He's good, said the fisherman. His son can find their boat in the dark.

Jason says he remembered the day his uncles finally agreed to teach him. He had impressed them, just like the fisherman's boy. He had walked down Seaside St. in Kaunakakai one Saturday to meet them on his own. The uncles, they had mentioned to his mother that they'd been asked to kōkua for a party. It had been a piece of a much larger conversation about the weekend, but Jason had heard it, and without telling his parents, he woke up early the next morning and met his uncles to help them pick up their nets.

This fishing, said the Miloliʻi fisherman. His father taught it to him. And his grandfather taught it to his father. The fisherman said it goes way back like this. He's at least the fifth generation.

Jason began to wonder what he was doing there. Not there listening to the fisherman, but there in the ballroom. He was all dressed up, ready to take it to the next level, he says. He was ready to learn about fishing from people who had studied fishing all their adult lives. From people who'd been qualified to make big decisions about Hawaiʻi's fisheries.

The Miloliʻi fisherman said when they get to the school of akule, it's him and his boy. They find the giant ball of fish in the dark because he's been taught where to find it. He doesn't really even have to look. Even if the school's just arrived in Miloliʻi, he knows where it is.

Maybe it was the fisherman's voice, Jason says. The way it had gotten louder and then seemed to crack. But soon there were others who stood up to leave, who picked up their conference bags and their binders, the handouts, and slid out their rows, down the aisle, and out the door at the back of the ballroom. This made Jason mad, he says. Distracted. Annoyed. Irritated. Here was a fisherman, like him, telling a story—a good one at that, finally—and these people were walking out as if no one could see them.

The fisherman stopped for moment to collect himself in a way that made Jason think something big was coming. The fisherman might snap because he came all that way, and like Jason, hadn't heard anything of much real use when it came to fishing in Miloliʻi. The fisherman was obviously uncomfortable up there—he was standing behind a podium and a microphone, in the front of a massive ballroom and more a thousand attendees. He was a fisherman, after all.

So it surprised Jason when the fisherman resumed talking as if he didn't see the people leaving the ballroom. The fisherman just continued, Jason says, with one last thing: When he's out on the ocean at times like those, he doesn't think much about fishing. He thinks instead about the bond between his son and the fish. He imagines the school of akule that migrates through Miloliʻi are the same fish, from the same school, that his own father took him to catch when he was a boy. He thinks of his grandfather and his grandfather's father. Then he imagines his son—now that he's there—has become part of a cycle that's older and truer than anything else he knows. A genealogy of man intimately connected to a genealogy of fish.

It was a moment of clarity.

Jason says he felt something come over him when the fisherman said this. It was right then, he says, that he wanted to stand up. He was charged. He clenched his fists and leaned forward in his chair. He was going to applaud. But then, he says, in the moment of silence, the fisherman turned from the podium and made his way to his seat.

Jason looked around. The ballroom wasn't full anymore.

Before he knew it, people were standing up to leave, even the fisherman.

I don't believe Jason when he says this, but he tells me he cried. He brought his hands to his face, and cried right there in his seat. He stayed there until it was quiet. He didn't know what he was going to do.

After a few minutes, when he had cleaned himself up, he walked out the ballroom and into the lobby. He saw people in line, smiling at each other, chatting, on their way to the buffet. He hadn't eaten all morning, but now he wasn't hungry. He kept walking through the lobby until he was on a balcony of the hotel overlooking the Ala Wai Harbor. He was standing there, looking out above all the cars lining the street, beyond the boats docked in the slips, toward the horizon. He stood there for some time before he finally moved, and when he did, he says he finally saw me.

I was right there below him, maybe a hundred yards away. I was sitting in a boat, docked right there beside the 'Ilikai. I'd just crossed the channel with some boys from Mana'e. We'd been escorting a canoe all morning. I raised my hand and yelled, "Moloka'i!" And all the boys in the boat looked up and yelled it again.

Jason raised a fist in the air, then left the railing on the balcony. Within a few minutes, he was standing above us on the pier, taking shots from the boys because of his slacks and his shoes. We offered him food, and before I knew it, he was in the boat beside me. He'd taken off the aloha shirt. He had chopsticks in his hand and was poking at the fresh sashimi. "Brah," he said. "It's crazy up there. You wouldn't believe it." Then he started telling me his story.

I Kelat

Desiree Taimanglo-Ventura

The Fence. I Kelat.

It is wrapped around my mother's tongue, gagging her.

She spits mispronounced hope,
sounds fallen into disrepair from neglect.

It is wrapped around my wrists,

catching light,

reflecting off of walls,

    casting shadows,

        jingling as I write down grocery lists for relatives with no jewelry to call their own.

It's draped across the empty womb of a Yigo girl hailed an officer by backwater Alabamans, a jungle bunny turned "hero,"

hero turned victim,

victim turned

and still… turning.

It is tucked neatly in my wallet, waving me toward fluorescent lit aisles,
lined with Enfamil, cans of hard biscuits, and ground beef.

It even talks,

whispering legends of a freedom so oppressing that I bury my child in the margins,

making sure nothing is left, but a tombstone of footnotes.

It is taped on the windshield of my father's car, greeting skeptical blue eyes as he returns to a village fallen
through the cracks of gratitude,

Guiding his way past a cemetery filled with bones resting beneath his grandson's name.

I find it in yellowed albums,

showing up unexpectantly in manamko eyes and ignorant grins.

It even dances.

It cha cha'd at my wedding, beside officer's wives.
Gyrated beside girls thrown together under their father's last four.

It sleeps between my husband and I,

filling the night air with silent animosity,

Indignant thoughts about a boy born proud to be an American… from a girl raised provin' to be an American.

I kelat? The fence?

My bones have been gutted of calcium by "I kelat."

I brush flakes of rusted metal off a skeleton grown brittle with liberation.

102

kawaiaha'o

me ke aloha palena 'ole no ko kākou iwi kūpuna
Lufi A. Matā'afa Luteru

'auhea 'oukou e nā 'ōiwi?
a sound sleep does not exist
present are thieves and grave robbers
labeled as mere "bones" in a cemetery
a nuisance that impedes "progress"

Christian contradiction reveals
diseased holy vanity
insufferable addiction to
material impermanence
capitalism, preach to us

embrace 'ōiwi disconnection
"there is no life in the bones"
e "kahu", wahahe'e nō 'oe! tsā!
our kūpuna are prisoners
ancestors desecrated

disturbed and displaced
in a musky basement
in a church of "god"
preach love and live
an eternal farce

utter travesty exudes as
we view, through rusty metal gates
under lock and key
iwi kupuna treated as criminals
tears inconsolably flow

as reassuring Jezebel promises are whispered
"eternal peace" exists for the children of the "Lord"
really? what a contradiction!

colonial powers dictate to us
we are not important

"unmarked" equals archaic sacred less?
haole self-serving justification
through devious smiles
false authority exudes
absolute sacrosanct

eternal maggots invade
a forever fester
lies consume
patronizing us
like a modern Bingham with brown skin

capitalism continually breeds
a shift to intolerably
askew and separate us from
our identity as kānaka maoli
know this, our iwi kūpuna are not dispensable

we live, they live

Rejuvenation
ma ka mahina ʻo Māhealani, ma ke one o Mākua
Lufi A. Matāʻafa Luteru

kau ka lā i ka lolo
activate and renew
this humble vessel
weary and weighed upon
naʻau yearns to release
troubled churning contained
beating heavily upon
my sunburned shoulders
dehydrated and aged kuahu
revive moʻoʻōlelo ripened
retaining life sacred
reminder of
Haumea's abundant gift
of fertility overflowing
growing seeds of
consciousness
brilliantly lit
nightsky abound
Hina's glory eternal
glow tranquilly presides
over mighty Kanaloa
ebb and flow
amniotic wai
antiquity sync within
a flowering womb
feel the refreshing cool
penetration of salty sea
surround me and
powerfully embrace
this humble offering
as bitter waters blend
and ascend to the heavens
with prayers of peace

awestruck witness to
wondrously rare
ānuenue pō
lipo like blackened kukui
embedded within my skin
kapu pathway
quietly gliding
arch of Ka'ena
ever so soft
loving light
reaching upwards silently
as we long to journey
back to our ancestors

My Mother's Bamboo Bracelets: A Handful of Lessons on Saving the World

Julian Aguon

*A speech given at the Commencement Exercises of the William S.
Richardson School of Law Honolulu, Hawai'i, May 17, 2009*

Si Yu'us Ma'åse' and thank you Chief Justice Richardson, deans, faculty,
regents, alumni, friends, family and loved ones, for joining us tonight
as we celebrate this year's graduating class of our fine William S.
Richardson School of Law.

Dear classmates: Thank you. It is an honor to be able to share some of
my thoughts with you on this beautiful evening.

I have thought of you so often in the last several weeks, as I have
meandered the landscapes of my mind to figure out what I could
possibly say that could be of use to you. You have no idea how much
I've agonized over constructing my talk away from my usual bullets:
human rights, self-determination, demilitarization. You'll be impressed.
I have, for the most part, succeeded. But, as a writer, I know that nothing
of worth can be written that is not culled from the light of my own life.
So bear with this writer-activist from Guam, as I relay twelve minutes
worth of what I have come to know of the world. Hopefully, you can take
something of what is imparted with you in the new morning. If not, feel
free to throw it out a high window.

Despite what we've been told, the world is not ours for the taking.
Indeed, the world we have inherited comes to us bruised, a tender shard
of her former self, having passed clumsily through the well-intentioned
hands of our mothers and fathers, seeking, seeking a generation it can
trust enough, and long enough, to drop its shoulders.

Of the belief that love can save the world, I have a story to tell: In the
old days in the land now known as Guam, when the people lost their
connection to their way, when the rains would not come and the people
grew wild with hunger, a giant grouper fish determined to destroy Guam

began to eat the island widthwise, one giant chunk after another. Day after day, the men of Guam tried to stop it. They pursued it with spears, tried in vain to trap it, to catch it with nets they had made. They called upon the ancestors to aid in the capture. Every day, the women of Guam offered to help catch the giant fish, and every day the men, forgetting the strength of women, rejected them. One night, while the women were weaving the pandanus leaves, the answer came to the *maga'håga*, the elder and leader among them. The women would weave a giant net from their long black hair. One by one, the women, old and young, came forward, knelt on the black stone, and parted with their beauty. Then they got to work, weaving and chanting through the night. By first light, they finished the net and set the trap. Though the giant fish convulsed violently, it could not break it. Imbued with the women's intention, it was woven with deep spiritual affection and was therefore unbreakable. However, the women could not haul the giant fish ashore alone. When the men heard what was happening, they rushed to help the women and, together, they hauled the fish ashore. Its meat was shared with everyone.

They say it was our women's offering of beauty that saved Guam.

It has taken me many years to understand what this story is about, and why it is still passed down so many millennia later. I am convinced that its lessons, which have served my own people well, may be of some use to us today, as we look out at a world whose contours give us pause, and make us feel at times as if whatever we do, whatever we are, will not be enough.

But, and here's the first lesson, no offering is too small. No stone unneeded. All of us, whether we choose to become human rights attorneys or corporate counsel, or choose never to practice law at all, but instead become professors or entrepreneurs or disappear anonymous among the poor, or stay at home and raise bright, delicious children, all of us, without exception, are qualified to participate in the rescue of the world.

But this is a quiet truth, and quiet truths are hard to hear when the cynics are outside howling.

Like the women who wove their hair into a magic net, we also do well to remember that saving the world requires all of our *hands*. As a group that has largely chosen the life of the mind, this will be especially important to remember. It would be a great folly to think that our ideas, no matter how good, would be enough to reverse the dangerous, downward trajectory of our planet. As an activist on the ground, I have often suspected that it is harder for people to rush to the rescue of a world whose magic they have not encountered for themselves, have not seen, felt, touched, turned over in their own hands. I for one can say without pause that so large a part of my own devotion to the cause of justice is that I have hiked up my pants and stood in other peoples' rivers. Moved to their music. Carried their babies. Watched them come back from burying their dead.

Our next lesson is that any people who profess to love freedom permit others room. Room to grow, to change their mind, to mess up, to leave, to come back in. In our story, the women did not reject the men who had done the same to them. They accepted their help, welcomed it. True, they could not haul in the fish alone, and needed the men. But perhaps that is the whole unromantic, utterly useful point: the part, no matter how pure its intention, cannot save the whole. And I think this should not so much make us tentative, as it should anchor us in the reality of our collective vulnerability, in the immediacy of our connection.

So anchored, another truth becomes plain: it is strength, not power, that must be the object of our affection.

Finally, a word about beauty: I have been thinking about beauty so much lately. About folks being robbed of it, folks fading for want of it, folks rushing to embrace only ghosts of it.

There have been periods in my own life when my grief felt more real to me than my hope, moments when my rage, sitting up, threatened to swallow my softness forever. It is here, in these moments, in these fields where older versions of myself come to die, that I am forced again to clarify what exactly it is that I believe. For example, though so much of my energy of late has been in the service of opposing the largest military buildup in recent history, which is now underway in my home Guam,

I don't really believe that I am, that we are, going to stop the U.S. Defense Department from doing what it will. So what is it that I, that we, believe really?

In law school, we are taught early the importance of tight argumentation. We learn to revere the elegance of restraint. We become tailors who sew beautiful clothes of our reason. Somewhere along the way, we pick up a reflex. An intuitive feeling that we should only fight the fights we can win. Lawyer inside the narrowest possible nook.

But this is not *our* way. As lawyers fashioned in the William S. Richardson School of Law tradition, sharp analytical skills are not the only tools in our toolkit.

In our hands, we hold a *precious* version, passed carefully to us by our teachers, of what it means to be a lawyer, of how it looks to begin cool from the premise that the law is not neutral, and then thoughtfully, strategically, politically go about using it in the service of justice.

This is what I love most about Richardson. If we paid attention, even to the silences, we leave here knowing that it is not good enough just to go out and fight the fights we can win. Rather, Richardson nurtures in us a respect for possibilities and, when we are ready, gently says to us, even without saying, "go out and fight the fights that need fighting."

In the relay, something else, something so quiet it can barely be heard, is also transmitted. Let us look at it in the light.

Each of us who decides to engage in social change lawyering must find our own way to build an inner life against the possibility, and, a certain measure of inevitability, of failure. Indeed, part of our work as people who pattern our lives around this belief—this deep, daring belief—that what we love we can save, is to prepare our wills to withstand some losing, so that we may lose and still set out again, anyhow.

I for one, especially of late, feel like I'm at a funeral when I go home. I see her: Guam as a fishbowl for so many different kinds of dying. As many of you know, while here with you at law school, I have always been there, too. My focus, always split. Three years later, I can tell you: the pipes of everything I've wanted desperately to stop are being fitted and laid. Despite how wide our movement has grown, and how fiercely articulate the generation rising to challenge the changing tide, we are losing.

But then, if I am quiet enough, I hear them, trooping in: the women that taught me how to go about this business of keeping on keeping on. I hear them, all the sounds that saved my life: my mother's bamboo bracelets, back and forth on the kitchen counter, as she, after hours on her feet, gets dinner ready; the hooks on the bottom of my grandmother's net, dragging on the floor, as she comes back fishless from the sea; the steady hooves of Cec's horse, as she rides into the evening on the back of the only god she has left.

Having come from a tradition of beauty, of women's strength, of knowing what is worth wrapping one's arms around, I realize now that the most cherished of all things I am taking with me in the new morning is, quite simply, other people.

Good morning to you all, my friends, my colleagues, my co-workers. What I wish for you is that whatever work you do be, as they say, your love made visible. That, and, for your inner life, a good coat, because it can get very cold.

Congratulations Class of 2009. Your own small corners of the world are waiting for you.

Ponoiwi
Kapulani Landgraf

In 1907, the Hawaiian Commercial & Sugar Company constructed the Pā'ia lime kiln. H.C. & S. run by Alexander & Baldwin mined the coral sands from the beaches of Keonekapo'o to Pā'ia for seven decades. They manufactured hydrated lime for the processing of sugarcane and used the sand to construct roads and other buildings. In the mid-1940's, the United States Navy destroyed both Pu'u Hele and Pu'u Nēnē. Their cinders were quarried extensively to build roads and the air base at Pu'u Nēnē.

Historically, sand for the construction industry was often taken from beaches statewide. Honolulu Construction and Draying Company, Ltd. began taking sand from Pāpōhaku, Moloka'i in the early 1960's and shipped it to O'ahu. In 1972, the Hawai'i State Legislature banned sand mining operations below the high watermark. O'ahu concrete companies were forced into using "mansand," crushed basaltic rock but it was expensive and more difficult to use. They soon found a cheaper alternative, Maui dune sand. In 1985, the Leisure Estates were built on the sand dune of Waiehu. The sand was stockpiled until Ameron Hawai'i bought it and barged it to O'ahu. This marked the first shipment of Maui sand to O'ahu and it continues till today.

Native Hawaiians buried the iwi of their ancestors within the pu'u one (sand dunes) throughout Hawai'i. They believed the mana of the person lived in the bones. Ola nā iwi. The bones live. At Honokahua, Maui in 1989, over 1,000 Native Hawaiian remains were archaeologically disinterred to build the Ritz-Carlton Kapalua resort. As a result in 1990, the Hawai'i State Legislature passed Act 306, which provided a process in protecting known burial sites and established burial councils for each island. Despite this law, Hawaiian 'āina and iwi are constantly threatened by irresponsible development. Na wai e ho'ōla i nā iwi?

Ponoiwi Installation (detail)

Kapulani Landgraf

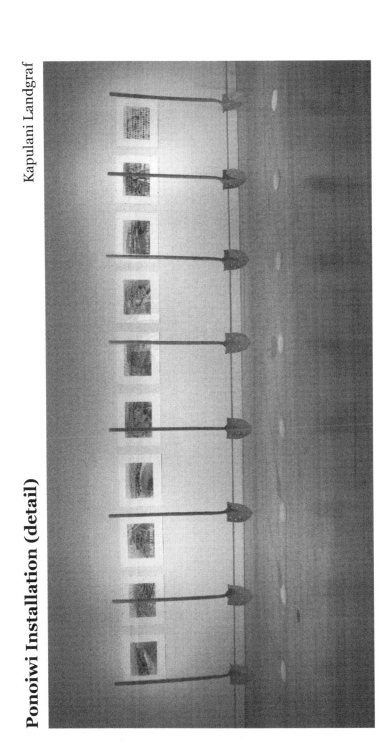

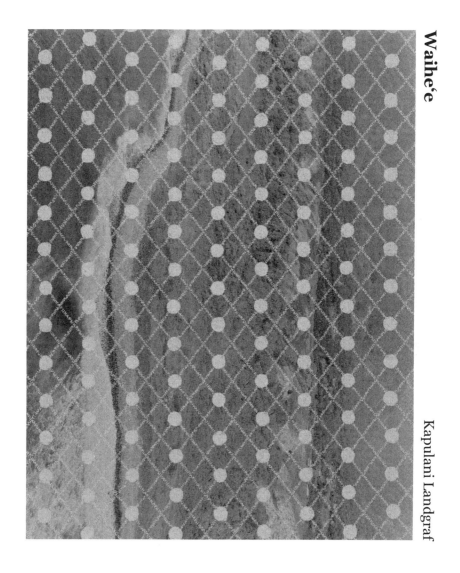

Waihe'e

Kapulani Landgraf

Pu'u Nēnē

Kapulani Landgraf

115

Kapukaulua

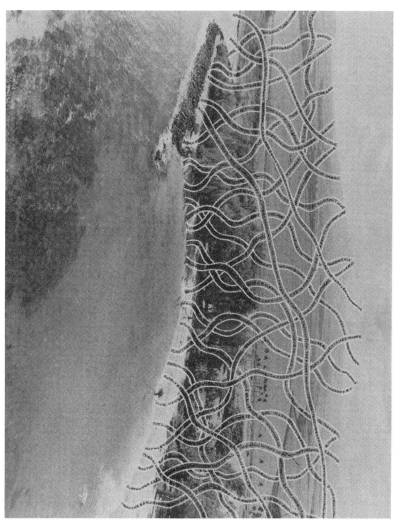

Kapulani Landgraf

Nā Hono a Piʻikea

Kapulani Landgraf

When I Give You a Jabong

Aiko Yamashiro

I wish you
anticipation
like citrus smell
blooming
like faith
to wait
holding
something
heavy that
grew hurt
and imperfect
long ago
I wish you
love.

I wish you bold
like peeling back
yellow skin
anxious scars
thick worry
like opening
a window
like finding a self
you stopped

believing in
like infinity
under a knife
I wish you
spilling

red pink
sea-star
spiraling
anemone
a pattern so
stunning you

want to spend
your life
separating
the membrane
from that
tender color
you want

to offer all
your sweet-
sour sunlight
to the ones
you love.

mai ka pō mai
for wayne kaumuali'i westlake
Donovan Kūhiō Colleps

a bent coconut midrib

arc

hive

AN ORGANISM. THE SECRET
ION OF AN ORGANISM. THE
SECRETION OF AN ORGAN
ISM. THE SECRETION OF AN

LISTENLISTENLISTENLISTENLISTENLISTENLISTENLISTENLISTENLISTENLISTEN

HE INOA NO KE KAHU MĀLAMA O NĀ ALA HELE WĀWAE O WAIKĪKĪ

'ĀINA

the   page   is

my   lo'i   the

page   **MAI**   my

lo'i   **KA**   page

is   **PŌ**   lo'i

our   **MAI**   grow

    pages

KA
'OIA'I'O

pala-pala

EA

120

Contributors

Aata is a multimedia artist and writer who exists in printmaking, photography, video, audio and sculpture. Her practice also involves non-traditional materials in forms such as inflatable structures and large scale pop-up books. Aata has been awarded the Heide Student Fund for Research and Special Art Projects, Honolulu, Hawaii, and her work has been exhibited at various venues, including the Oahu Fringe Fest, Kennedy Theater at University of Hawaii at Mānoa, and the ARTS at Marks Garage. Her new work will be featured in Pōuliuli, showing at the Yirramboi festival and ARTSPACE NZ in summer 2017. She holds a Bachelor of Visual Arts in Photography from the University of Hawaii at Mānoa.

Julian Aguon is a hybrid writer-activist-attorney whose work has taken the forms of polemical prose, poetry, law articles, academic lectures, and speeches. His scholarship principally concerns international human rights law and the rights of non-self-governing and indigenous peoples. He teaches International Law and works as an attorney in private practice.

Born and raised on the windward side of Oʻahu, **Ashlee Lena Affonso** has received both her Bachelor's (English and Political Science) and Master's degree (Political Science) from the University of Hawaiʻi at Mānoa. Her future aspirations include voyaging the South African coast, trekking through the cities of Brazil, and dipping her toes in the Aegean and Mediterranean Seas. But for now, she is currently a resource teacher at Kapālama Elementary School, and resides in the beautiful town of Kāneʻohe.

Tammy Hailiʻōpua Baker is an associate professor in the Department of Theatre and Dance at the University of Hawaiʻi at Mānoa. Her work centers on the development of an indigenous Hawaiian theatre aesthetic and form, Hawaiian language revitalization, and the empowerment of cultural identity through stage performance. Baker is also a playwright and the artistic director of Ka Hālau Hanakeaka, a Hawaiian medium theatre troupe. Originally from Kapaʻa, Kauaʻi she now resides in Kahaluʻu, Koʻolaupoko, Oʻahu.

Michael Lujan Bevacqua is an artist, activist, writer, blogger and father of two crazy Chamorro-speaking kids. His work deals with Guam's history of colonization and the possibilities and theories for its decolonization. In 2011 he led a successful effort to create a Chamorro Studies BA Program at the University of Guam.

Kisha Borja-Kicho'cho' is from Mangilao, Guam. She has taught at the secondary level and is currently teaching at the University of Guam. Her life's work is dedicated to her Mother(is)land, the place, people, and culture she comes from. Aside from teaching and engaging in meaningful projects, Kisha loves running and going on adventures with her husband Vito and their daughter Lina'la'.

Donovan Kūhiō Colleps is a Kanaka Maoli poet, student, and teacher from Pu'uloa, O'ahu. He teaches creative writing and composition at UH Mānoa. His poetry and prose have appeared in various publications in Hawai'i Nei, Aotearoa, and Turtle Island. His poetry collection, *Proposed Additions*, was published by Tinfish Press in 2014.

Born to Kalokeo Sarona Waiamau of Waipouli, Kaua'i and Gilbert D. Drexel of Coatsville, Pennsylvania, **April A.H. Drexel** is the youngest of four children. She has spent a lifetime within the ahupua'a of Wai'anae Uka (Wahiawā), and special hard core educational summers of her youth in Mākua, O'ahu. Drexel is perpetually A.B.D. in the field of History—specializing in Hawaiian, Pacific, American & World areas of concentration; received an M.F.A. (1989) and B.F.A. (1983)—in drawing & painting with an emphasis in Pacific Art History from UH Mānoa; completed an A.A. (1982)—in liberal arts with a particular focus in art (intaglio printing) & geography from Leeward Community College—Waiawa, O'ahu; a graduate of the Kamehameha Schools (1978)—Kapālama, O'ahu. Currently, Drexel is an Associate Professor at the Kamakakūokalani Center for Hawaiian Studies, Hawai'inuiākea School of Hawaiian Knowledge, UH Mānoa.

Alfred Peredo Flores is of Chamoru and Korean descent, born in Seoul, South Korea and raised in Southern California. He is currently a Ph.D. candidate in the Department of History at the University of CA, Los Angeles. He also received an M.A. in public history and a B.A. in history from the University of CA, Riverside. His specialization is 20th century U.S. history with an emphasis on U.S. empire, immigration, indigeneity, labor, and race/ethnicity. His research examines the post-World War II U.S. military expansion of Guam through empire, indigeneity, labor, and race. In addition to his scholarly pursuits, he is a co-founding member of the UCLA Graduate Coalition of the Native Pacific (GCNP) and Famoksaiyan, an organization committed to the decolonization of Guam.

Cara Flores-Mays is an indigenous Chamorro, a mother, a small-business owner, and an organizer for the grassroots organization "We Are Guåhan", which has played a significant role in educating the Guam community about the potential impacts of the proposed military buildup.

David Keali'i is a queer poet of mixed Kanaka Maoli descent born and raised in Western Massachusetts/Pocomtuc/Nipmuc territory. In 2009 he represented Worcester, Massachusetts at the 2009 National Poetry Slam. His work also appears in *'Ōiwi: A Native Hawaiian Journal, Mauri Ola: Contemporary Polynesian Poetry in English* (*Whetu Moana*, Volume II), *Assaracus*, and *Yellow Medicine Review*. His first collection of poems is forthcoming from Kuleana 'Ōiwi Press.

Kapulani Landgraf was born and lives in Pū'ahu'ula, Kāne'ohe. She currently is an Assistant Professor of Hawaiian Visual Art and Photography at Kapi'olani Community College, Kalāhū, Hawai'i.

Lufi A. Matā'afa Luteru is a native descendant of Hawai'i and Sāmoa. She is kupa'āina of Mākaha Valley, a proud single parent, cultural practitioner, educator, entrepreneur, poet, multi-media artisan, and lauhala weaver. She received her Masters degree in Hawaiian Studies and has taught Hawaiian Fiber Arts and Hawaiian Studies in the University of Hawai'i educational system for many years. She owns Pāwehi Creations and specializes in creating unique pāpale mo'olelo. Lufi currently has 4 pāpale mo'olelo of Haumea in the Bishop Museum. She also recently showcased her third pāpale collection based on the Kumulipo at the MAMo Wearable Art Show at the Hawai'i Theatre.

Selina Onedera-Salas is a Chamoru woman from Sinajana who is involved with various community projects for the perpetuation of the CHamoru language and for indigenous rights awareness. She is married to Vincent John Salas, and they have four sons: Rhico, Tristen, Matua, and Maga'låhi.

Jay Baza Pascua is a poet, writer, actor, storyteller, and Chamorro chanter. Jay told numerous news stories in his 15-year career as a journalist but now he passionately shares stories of his culture. He hopes his work inspires other Chamorros to embrace and perpetuate their heritage.

Michael Puleloa, Ph.D., was born on Majuro in the Marshall Islands and raised on Moloka'i in Hawai'i. He has taught English at Kapi'olani Community College and the University of Hawai'i at Mānoa. He is currently an English teacher at Kamehameha Schools, Kapālama, where he is also the advisor for *Ho'okumu*, the school's student literary journal. He has received awards for both his poetry and prose, and he has published in various literary journals in Hawai'i.

No'ukahau'oli Revilla is a creative writer based in Hawai'i. Born and raised on the island of Maui, she is currently pursuing a Ph.D. in the English program at the University of Hawai'i-Mānoa. Her chapbook *Say Throne* was published by Tinfish Press in 2011, and her poetry will be featured in the 2012 exhibition A Thousand Words and Counting at the Honolulu Museum of Art. No'u's next project is based on the city of Kahului in the 1950s.

Lyz Soto is Co-Executive Director of Youth Speaks Hawai'i and co-founder of Pacific Tongues, which are organizations committed to expanding and supporting spoken arts communities in Hawai'i and the Pacific. She has worked as the head coach of the Youth Speaks Hawai'i Slam Team since 2008 and she is currently working towards a PhD at University of Hawai'i at Mānoa in the Department of English, where she teaches English Composition, Introduction to Literature and Culture, and Introduction to Literature and Creative Writing. She has performed in venues and classrooms in Hawai'i and across the continental United States. Her chapbook, *Eulogies*, was published in 2010 by TinFish Press.

Desiree Taimanglo Ventura is a Chamoru author, educator, and activist from Yigo, Guam. She is currently an instructor of English and Communications at the Guam Community College. She has taught Undergraduate Composition at the University of Guam and Rhetoric at San Diego State University. She is also the author of the Guahan Mommy blog, which focuses on issues related to Chamoru women, decolonization, and raising Chamoru children.

Aiko Yamashiro's ancestors are fierce, broken, resilient, and loving Japanese, Okinawan, and Chamorro people, who she is continuing to humbly know as guides in her life as a poet, activist, student, and teacher of decolonial literatures of the Pacific. She is co-editor of *The Value of Hawai'i 2: Ancestral Roots, Oceanic Visions* (University of Hawai'i Press, 2014) and her poetry has been published in *Hawai'i Review, blackmail press,* and *Spiral Orb*.

Made in the USA
San Bernardino, CA
07 January 2018